HEAVENLY HUGS

Comfort,
Support, and
Hope From
the Afterlife

HEAVENLY
HUGS

CARLA WILLS-BRANDON, PhD

New Page Books
A division of The Career Press, Inc
Pompton Plains, N.J.

HEAVENLY HUGS
EDITED AND TYPESET BY KARA KUMPEL
Cover design by Joseph Sherman/Dutton and Sherman Design
Printed in the U.S.A. by Courier

Unless otherwise indicated, all identifying details in the personal stories have been been changed to protect privacy.

To order this title, please call toll-free 1-800-CAREER-1 (NJ and Canada: 201-848-0310) to order using VISA or MasterCard, or for further information on books from Career Press.

The Career Press, Inc.
220 West Parkway, Unit 12
Pompton Plains, NJ 07444
www.careerpress.com
www.newpagebooks.com

Library of Congress Cataloging-in-Publication Data

CIP Data Available Upon Request.

This work is dedicated to my soul mate, Michael, and my angels, Aaron and Joshua.

ACKNOWLEDGMENTS

HEAVENLY HUGS is the end product of many creative endeavors. In placing my titles with the right publishers, my good friend and agent John White never ceases to amaze me. I love you, John. You are my literary and spiritual rock. Presenting this particular book to Michael Pye, senior acquisitions editor for New Page Books, was just the right call. Both he and Adam Schwartz, acquisitions editor, were incredibly supportive. Thank you for taking me on!

Senior developmental editor Kirsten Dalley provided the fine-tuning for my words. Her gentle guidance was invaluable, while line editor Kara Kumpel and editor Gina

Talucci gave this work its final polishing. What would I do without great editors?! You are both so appreciated.

When I first saw the book cover, I gave Jeff Piasky two thumbs up! His beautifully crafted work was stunning. Also, like most writers I'm lousy at promoting my titles. Thankfully, Laurie Kelly-Pye, director of sales and publicity, is a pro. She made it easy! Kate and Simon Warwick-Smith of Warwick Associates were then able to use their creativity and introduce this title to readers.

My incredible photographer friend Manny Chan once again made me look better than I do in real life! Creative web designer Dr. Keith Bly, who hides under the guise of a pediatric specialist at a major medical school, took care of my needs at the drop of a hat. The "witch" thanks you!

Dr. Erlendur Haraldsson, one of the original deathbed vision researchers, has been a true friend and mentor. Upon his shoulders I stand. Australia's Victor Zammit is another buddy of mine and he has always supported my work. This is a "we" not "me" deal.

To the many dear experiencers who have bravely shared with me their departing vision accounts I say thank you from the bottom of my heart. Your openness will comfort others. Some have passed on to the afterlife. Then there are those of you who do not want to be identified publicly. Though I have taken great care to protect your identities, know I carry who you really are within my soul at all times.

Finally and most importantly is my loving family. My husband, Michael, has lived with a crazy author for decades and he knows the drill well. When I'm writing a book, he picks up the slack. The grill comes out and I'll find him in the backyard preparing the evening meal.

My boys, Aaron and Joshua, step in to set the table and take care of the dishes. Along with this, they all tolerate me if I go off the deep end. When it comes right down to it, without the love and support of my dear family I wouldn't be able to write. I love you guys.

CONTENTS

PREFACE

We Never Die Alone

Of course you don't die. Nobody dies. Death doesn't exist. You only reach a new level of vision, a new realm of consciousness, a new unknown world.

—Henry Miller

PHYSICAL DEATH IS NOT THE END

No matter what your religion, spiritual tradition, or philosophy, know that physical death is not the end. As we cross the threshold separating this life from the next, we will not be alone. Reunited with dear ones who have already bridged the gap between this life and the next, fear quickly fades, and joy fills our hearts.

For proof, read this account of a departing vision—the first of many you will find in this book—about a beloved husband and father.

My husband bravely fought many hard medical battles. When my spirits were down he would encourage me to have faith. He was such a trooper. For a time it looked as though he'd turned a corner, but then his battered body finally gave up. In the end the doctors told us all we could do was hope for a miracle. When I heard that nothing more could be done I was completely devastated. My whole life had been about my marriage and my family. Death was stealing him from me and I felt like I was losing a limb. The pain was unbearable. I wondered how I would continue without my best friend. My children didn't know what to do. Their father had always been their rock. They were having a difficult time with the news, and I could tell they were worried about me too.

As my husband's illness progressed, the tables turned and it was I who became the cheerleader, encouraging him to hang in there. I didn't give up hope until the very end.

One day I came to his room bringing another in a series of strange cures, and my poor husband said to me, "Enough." After months of medical treatments, nutritional supplements, protein smoothes, numerous hospitalizations, and harsh drugs, I knew I had to begin to let him go.

My handsome husband of so many years was physically becoming a shell of his former self, and I finally realized he was tired. Once I admitted to myself that my need for him to stay alive was making his remaining time more difficult, I stopped pushing. He had run out of fight, was making peace with his impending death, and it was time for me to support his decision. After that, our last days together ended up bringing us closer.

Hospice was wonderful. I don't know how any of us would have made it without their loving support and care. Not only were they there for my husband, making him comfortable and managing his pain, but the concern they showed me and my children was amazing. My friends were also supportive, especially when I felt I couldn't go on. When I thought my heart would break, they would hug me and let me just sob.

Not knowing how many days, hours, or minutes we had left, I moved into my husband's room. As his death drew nearer he began sleeping more, but periodically he was very lucid. During those times we would fondly remember our history together and the kids' childhood years. We also said all of the things we had neglected to say during better days, like, "I love you," and "I'm sorry." We tied up loose ends, and discussed his funeral and how I'd survive once he was gone. He then wanted to talk about what happens to us after we die. To ignore this would have put a barrier between us. After all was said and done, we watched dumb programs on television and listened to the music of our youth.

When he finally stopped eating I knew the end was very near.

One afternoon I needed to go home and check on our pets. My husband was resting comfortably and the hospice team assured me they would call immediately if there were any changes. After taking care of some business at the house and grabbing something to eat, I returned to my husband to find a very concerned nursing staff. Before I entered his room, the hospice team said they wanted to talk with me. They said he had been acting very strangely, and wildly waving his hands around. I asked, "Waving his hands? Are you sure he's not agitated, or in pain?" With this they replied, "No, not at all. That's why his behavior seems so odd to us."

I then looked in on my husband and was shocked at what I saw. He wasn't waving his hands around and he definitely wasn't upset. If anything, he was happy. Looking closer I gasped. Turning to the nurses, I said, "Oh my goodness, he's using sign language!" The nurses then asked, "Why would he use sign language?" and I replied, "Because both of his parents were deaf from birth and this is how he communicated with them."

Surprised, they asked, "Are his parents still alive?" Smiling, I said, "No, they passed on years ago, but it looks as though they have returned for him."

INTRODUCTION

Departing visions, also known as deathbed visions (or DBVs), come in all shapes and sizes. Some people receive visitations from deceased relatives, whereas others encounter angels or religious figures. Those who are about to physically die will often talk about seeing beautiful landscapes on the other side, stating that this is where they will be after they pass. In most cases, once a dying person has had such a vision, death is no longer something for him or her to fear. Later, family, friends, and healthcare professionals at the bedside sometimes see a wisp of "something" leaving the body at the moment of passing.

These phenomena are nothing new. They have been described over and over again, for as long as time can remember. Throughout the book I will be presenting many personal accounts of departing visions and afterlife communications, demonstrating that our friends and family now living in spirit will be there for us when this life ends. The departing vision brings comfort not only to the dying, but also to those who love them, and even dreams can be the doorway to a heavenly hug.

As we begin to explore the departing vision, a simple analogy might help. By looking at any form of afterlife contact as a spiritual postcard, news clip, or telephone greeting from another dimension, these encounters will begin to make more sense to us. Physicists have been investigating the possibility of the existence of other dimensions for several centuries. Perhaps the departing vision is simply a sort of communication via a bridge between two realties: this life and the next. Can those who have shed their physical bodies and left this earthly plane now move back and forth from one dimension of existence to another?

Western culture begins telling our children at a very early age that any form of afterlife communication is the stuff of fantasy stories, make-believe, and myth. By the time most kids hit adolescence they have been convinced by teachers, clergy, parents, and other adults that our three-dimensional state of existence is all there is.

As adults, many of us have learned to dismiss the possibility of alternate realities, especially when such ideas don't fit in with our cultural and religious norms. It's now time to return to that childlike state of awe. We can reclaim the spirituality of our youth by keeping an open mind. In doing this, we will become even more receptive to receiving messages of love from our friends and relatives living in the next dimension.

This is my message to you. Now it's time to see what other experiencers have to say.

CHAPTER 1

Finding Answers

Death ends a life, not a relationship.
—Jack Lemmon

The Fourth of July evening festivities had started out with a bang—a big one. My family and I were spending the holiday at our small cabin in the wooded Smoky Mountains of North Carolina. Friends had joined us for thick shrimp gumbo, fudge brownies, and fireworks. The air was cool and the smell of magnolias competed with the scent of evergreens. That night, even the typical stormy summer weather was cooperating.

The clouds had parted, allowing the twinkle of star-light to peek through. Down the mountain, the village community had finished blowing up an arsenal of multi-colored fireworks. As the smell of gun powder dissipated, my oldest son yelled, "Now it's time for the home show!"

As fiddle music down in the village floated to the top of the mountain, out of the trunk of our car appeared the kid-sparklers and brightly packaged firecrackers. With each strike of a match a loud explosion would ricochet off one mountain to the next. The repetitious, "Boom! Boom! Boom!" sounded like cannons firing, and with this the ghosts of the past must surely have stirred. It was as if the Civil War had erupted in the South again.

Though my husband and the boys jumped for joy, with each loud bang my nerves began to feel frazzled. After an explosion, I'd say a prayer to the loving spirit of my mother: "Please protect each little toe and finger."

Eventually, all the small bombs had been blown to bits. My youngest boy then tugged on my shirt and asked, "Are there any more?" I drew in a sigh of relief and said, "Talk to your father." I then headed indoors for a soothing cup of tea. This rattled mother was in need of a break.

As I opened the door to the cabin, I noticed one of my friends had the television on. The TV was small and the picture was very grainy. "That's weird," I thought. "She's sitting in here all by herself." She was watching a well-known Hollywood psychic take requests from a studio audience. Questions like, "My father just died; can you contact him for me?" and, "Do you see my grand-mother? Does she have a message for me?" were bringing tears to her eyes. I knew who this particular psychic was and didn't have much regard for what I was hearing.

I've had the pleasure of knowing some very trustworthy mediums and psychics who were committed to helping others. Sadly, this guy wasn't one of them. Looking at my friend, I wondered why she was watching such nonsense while the rest of us were outside celebrating.

As I began preparing myself a cup of tea, I heard the television psychic make a pitch to the audience for his set of books, CDs, and services. The studio cameras then panned across the paranormal guru's devotees. Grief-stricken mothers, fathers, wives, husbands, daughters, and sons, several with tears running down their cheeks, willingly pulled out their checkbooks to purchase hundreds, even thousands of dollars worth of products.

As my friend continued to watch this sales pitch, her tears dried up and the hypnotic pull of the program suddenly dissolved. Shaking her head, she finally noticed I was standing in the room and said, "That's just terrible." Joining her on the couch I asked, "What's wrong?" With the click of the remote the television screen went blank. She laid back, sighed, and said, "What that psychic was doing is wrong. First, he's taking financial advantage of a group of folks in serious grief." With a look of exasperation she continued, "Secondly, what he's saying to several people in the audience doesn't make any sense to them. When told his messages from the 'departed' are way off base, he argues and tells the grieving they are wrong. Wouldn't relatives and friends know more about their deceased loved ones than this guy?"

After tossing a pillow across the room she added, "Telling these poor people they don't know what they were talking about adds to their grief. It's just not right." After this sudden, surprising explosion of emotion she looked out the open door. Following her gaze, I saw she was watching the kids running down the mountain waving sparklers. Concerned, I turned back to my friend, and saw the tears were welling up in her eyes again.

After I handed her a tissue, she continued. "That psychic's behavior is really reprehensible, but his show did remind me of something. It's an experience I haven't really told anyone about." Outside, my husband and the boys had found a few more bottle rockets and the fire-cracker war was on, but my friend didn't even notice. Instead, she surprised me by saying, "I had some strange experiences with my mom, before and just after she died." In spite of the renewed rounds of cherry bomb blasts, the teary-eyed woman sitting on my couch had my full attention.

"Mom was the nurturer and the anchor in the family," she said. "She supported me through not only a rough divorce, but also my battle with cancer. We talked to each other several times a day and even vacationed together. Mom and I had more fun!" Remembering the closeness she felt with her mother brought a smile to her face, but as she continued to talk it became obvious her distress wasn't only about her grief.

"Several days before my mother died, she started talking about going home. When I told her she was already at home, she looked past me and said, 'No, I want to go home! I want to go over there!' I don't think Mom was talking about the home she lived in on Peach Street. I think she was talking about heaven!" Having heard numerous accounts just like this from the dying, I nodded in agreement.

"I was at my house when she finally passed. At the time of her death I felt her squeeze my shoulder, just like she use to do when I was a kid. When I turned around, no one was there. Several minutes later the phone rang and it was my sister telling me Mom had died."

My friend's mother had experienced a departing vision. She had caught a glimpse of the afterlife just before she left her physical body. Then, at the moment of passing, the daughter had been touched by her mother's spirit. After I handed my friend one more tissue, she dried her eyes and continued. "After Mom died, I knew she was no longer suffering and was now in heaven with my grandparents, but I still felt so sad. The depression was debilitating. I couldn't work, stopped taking care of myself, and felt as though life had lost its meaning. All I did was cry and I didn't know who to talk to."

"Then I had a wild dream," she said. "Mom came to me in a dream. This dream was like nothing I'd ever experienced before. It was so real, so unlike my normal dreams." After taking a sip of her tea she put down her cup and shared with me an after-death communication. "At the end, Mom just wasn't herself. She had lost a ton of weight and was so terribly thin. Illness had ravaged her body and I prayed for her misery to end quickly. Well, in the dream Mom was her old self again and she had come to tell me she was just fine. Just like old times, Mom was dolled up from head to toe. Her hair was perfect, her nails were beautifully manicured, and she was wearing her usual shocking-red lipstick." Laughing, she added, "In the dream she gave me a great big hug and I could even smell her awful fruity perfume!" For a moment my friend was silent, back in the past. She was reliving her dream, remembering this sweet reunion. After a couple of minutes, she shook herself back to the present and then returned to her tale.

"I tried talking to my minister about my mom's visions before she died, and he told me I'd misinterpreted her words. That she was just confused. Then I told him about the dream I had after she died, how real it was, and he said this was just my grief! The guy wouldn't even listen to me when I tried to explain to him I'd never had a dream like that before in my life! I left his office feeling more upset than ever.

"After asking a few of my friends what they thought, most of them just looked at me like I was nuts. One very religious woman from work even accused me of 'consorting with unclean spirits'! That left me feeling very freaked out. I quickly stopped talking about it with any of them. Guess I should have known better. The biggest mistake I made was asking my therapist about all of this. I told him what my mom had said about 'going home' before she died. He told me Mom didn't see heaven. Instead, he blamed the vision on her brain dying. Then he gave me a big speech on how the brain fires off all of these neurons when a person is about to die. He said she was either confused or hallucinating.

"When I asked him what he thought about me feeling her squeeze my shoulder before I knew she had died, he said I was 'distraught.' As for the dream, after hearing about that, he then referred me to a psychiatrist for medication! After the session, I just sat in my car and cried for 30 minutes."

More tears slid down her face as I gently reached over and hugged her. I then reassured her that I believed everything she had just told me. Feeling comforted, she added, "I really believe my mother is just fine, but why is everyone brushing me off as some grief-stricken woman who isn't thinking straight? I can't find anyone who believes me. I went to friends, the minister, and my therapist, and they all rationalized my experiences and left me feeling crazy. I'm not off my rocker and I don't need medication. What I've needed is for someone to really listen to me and take what I say seriously. You are the first person to tell me my experiences are real!"

Wiping her eyes one more time, she then clicked on the remote and there again was the Hollywood psychic promoting more books, newsletters, and individual healing sessions by telephone. With the slickness of a salesman he continued hawking his wares to the newly bereaved. For a few seconds I was confused as to why my friend had turned the television back on. Then it hit me. She was looking for answers and wondering if anyone else had ever had such experiences. My believing her was a start, but it wasn't going to be enough.

With this "light bulb" realization, I hugged her again. My happiness for her heavenly hugs had been mixed with sadness. The departing visions and after-death communication comforted her, but in searching for answers she continued to feel misunderstood and overwhelmed. After being dismissed by the people she trusted the most, she was fearful of ever sharing again. My friend had been brave to confide in me. Though I was glad she had taken the risk to share her remarkable afterlife experiences with me, I also knew she still needed more information. The TV psychic wasn't going to be her solution.

Finding Answers Can Be Hard

We live in a death-phobic society. Like so many of us, my dear friend had been totally unprepared emotionally and spiritually for her mother's passing. Major societal institutions, such as education, family, and religion, had never taught her how to sort out experiences like this.

Not only did she want me to be there for her, to hear about her extraordinary contact with her mother, but she also needed supportive reassurance that she wasn't alone. Along with this, she desperately required help in understanding what it was she had witnessed and felt. It was going to be essential for her to learn how to integrate these powerful, life-altering events into her everyday living experience.

After my friend dried her eyes, I smiled, and took both of her hands in mine. Glancing at the television psychic, I said, "That's definitely not spiritual, but your experiences with your mom are. I'm going to share with you a similar story about my own mother, mother-in-law, and father-in-law. Believe me, I've been in your shoes. My story will help you understand you aren't alone and that your encounters are more common than you think."

Taking the remote from her hand, I said "bye-bye" to the celebrity psychic, and once again the television was silenced.

CHAPTER 2

Pulling the Departing Vision out of the Closet

The dead are merely the countrymen of my future.
—Dean Koontz

Very few of the spiritual gems I've been sharing with you come from psychics or mediums. They make their way to me through people just like my friend who was watching the TV psychic on July 4th: Messages of reported contact with the afterlife fly through cyberspace and land in my e-mail inbox on a regular basis. I regularly receive phone calls or end up in live Internet chats with experiencers. Such was the case not long ago while

I was appearing on an international radio program, and Dr. Ron, a physician-turned-minister, called the show to share his thoughts on the departing vision. He then followed up with this note:

> As someone who has been in the practice of healing, I wanted to say what I could on the topic of dying, death, and departing visions. It's a shame the death and dying process has been reduced to such an industrial process. Death has become a sterile sort of commercial enterprise....

Dr. Ron is so right! With industrialized medicine the human touch is on the verge of extinction. Rarely do we die in the comfort of our own beds, surrounded by dear friends and family with our favorite pet beside us. The experience of death has become very antiseptic. When my mother passed, she did so by herself in a sterile hospital room, hooked up to a multitude of tubes. Because of hospital policy, I was too young to visit her, so family and friends had to sneak me in to say goodbye.

My grandfather died alone in a nursing home, in a shared room without any familiar comforts. Just before he passed a college friend of mine went to his bedside with a cell phone so that I could speak to him. The emptiness I felt as I said "I love you" was heartbreaking. My sadness was not so much about his passing as it was about the conditions in which he was leaving this life.

Concern over how we as a society deal with death is something I hear about all of the time. Death and dying has become an industry. Outside of the hospice movement, little has been done to change this. The process of dying should be a spiritual experience not only for the individual who is about to pass, but also for those who love and care for them.

In response to the way our culture deals with death and dying, my friend Dr. Ron also shared with me some of his experiences in the emergency room of a hospital.

The now-governor of the state was then the senior emergency room physician, and one night a 75-year-old man went flatline on the table, was coded, and came back and told us about his DBV (deathbed vision), and then laid down and died again. Well, we coded him again, and he came back to life, sat up, and told us to let him go. After that, he laid down and died once again. I was saddened that his wife was kept out in the waiting area. She missed what we saw and heard from her husband. I was even more saddened that another physician brushed off my inquiry as to what that experience meant to him....

I certainly have questioned why more clinicians seem to steadfastly ignore this topic. Working as a hospitalist is like working in a factory; again, our medical profession fits the industrial process, and as an employee of the factory, we are not at liberty to discuss the "failure rate" or the "flaws" in the production lines.

Dr. Ron's experiences as an ER physician validate why so many of us are unable to talk openly about our departing visions. The dying man in the previous account had an afterlife experience, was ready to die, and even asked the hospital staff to let him go, but they didn't listen to him.

Science's Skeptics

The world of science continues to be at odds with that of spirituality. Skeptical thinkers scoff at tales of departing visions, calling them superstitions, hallucinations, or the wishful thinking of those individuals who fear death. Such scientific skeptics aren't the only barrier to the open discussion of afterlife encounters; mental health professionals also shy away from such discussion during therapy sessions.

Many of my peers and colleagues have been judgmental of my investigations. I've been publicly ridiculed by skeptics and nonbelievers on numerous occasions, and at times, even members of the media have portrayed me as some sort of "flake." Watching this from the sidelines my close friends often ask me, "Why do you continue to dedicate years of your life to exploring these spiritual reunions?" My reasons for doing so are very simple. Professionally, I strongly believe that those who experience departing visions are no longer plagued by a fear of death. Because of this they are able to resolve issues of grief and loss in a healing manner. I want to support these experiencers. Currently, there are limited resources for those who seek out validation after such encounters.

Personally, my own otherworldly encounters with deceased friends and relatives have helped me grow spiritually. I started having departing visions and after-death communications when I was just 15. These treasured experiences continue to this day. When blessed with such contact I'm reassured that love never ends. With no fear of death, I now understand dying is just part of the journey to the next adventure.

In the early days, any form of spiritual contact left me with a great deal of uncertainty. This confusion forced me to break out of my rigidity as a professional and then sent me for answers as a seeker. In order to begin this journey I first had to be willing to reevaluate my spiritual beliefs and my views on religion, life, death, and the afterlife. Traveling this path I opened myself up to other afterlife experiences. This created even more questions. With an increasing number of encounters it was necessary to find other experiencers who were just like me. With support and validation, I no longer felt overwhelmed or upset when skeptics refused to hear me. Instead, I began to realize they had their own spiritual road to follow. And every once in a while such paths cross mine.

WATCHING A DYING SKEPTIC DEAL WITH AN AFTERLIFE ENCOUNTER

When experiencers share an account with me, I'm often the first person they have ever opened up to. Once I let them know that they haven't frightened me off, I then talk about some of my own afterlife encounters. My favorite personal accounts involve my own family, and I always start with the worst skeptic of the bunch: my beloved mother-in-law!

The year was 2002. It was a dark and gloomy day on the Gulf coast, but Mom's room was cramped and overheated. As I sat with my very ill mother-in-law, little did I know I was about to witness an unbelievable event.

She had decided to stop eating and wasn't taking in any liquids. With this, I knew death was near. Forcing nutrition on a person who is dying actually makes the process more difficult, so my husband and I were bound and determined to respect her wishes. Fighting with medical staff insistent on feeding her left us feeling extremely frustrated. Once Mom began describing visitations from unseen visitors, we knew she was almost ready to go and we were glad we had stuck to our guns.

Some hospice workers are familiar with the departing vision, but the woman sitting next to Mom's bedside didn't have a clue. The poor gal began to emotionally unravel as my mother-in-law started having animated discussions with her invisible visitors. Immediately, medications for hallucinations were strongly suggested and the doctor was called. Sadly, the hospice worker didn't realize this common, comforting spiritual event was more potent than any pill.

During a departing vision the dying will often describe those invisible visitors they are communicating with. For experiencers, the visions are very real and they respond as they would to someone visible to everyone in the room. Some experiencers become extremely confused or even angry when others at the bedside don't acknowledge who it is they are seeing.

Though I understood the departing-vision phenomenon inside and out, I never dreamed this would be part of my skeptical mother-in-law's exit script!

Mom was a scientifically minded professor with not one but two PhDs. A radical, hardcore feminist, always dressed in stylish heels and high fashion, she believed an evening devoted to arguing politics was a good time! Discussions about pop culture, the afterlife, or religion were a waste of brain cells. When my first book on the spiritual experiences of the dying was published, she didn't rush to read it. My mother-in-law let me know right away that she had no time for what she called "superstitious nonsense."

One could confidently say she was incredibly cynical about all things spiritual, and for good reasons: In her early 20s Mom lost her own mother to the Nazi death camps in Poland. After such a loss her questions were, "Why did I survive?" and "How could six million have been murdered? Why would a kind God let this happen?" Because of her tragic history she rejected spiritual matters for decades, but my husband, Michael, and I often talked about how wonderful it would be if Mom had a reunion with her own mother at the moment of her physical death. After such discussions we'd look at one another and shake our heads no. Both of us were convinced she would go out kicking and screaming.

Sitting at my mother-in-law's bedside as her frail body gave way, I learned that even skeptical university professors can be surprised. On the morning of her passing, Mom was very irritated. She didn't understand her departing visions. Her sister was with us and the two were deep in conversation. In Polish my mother-in-law said, "These scenes are annoying!

Crazy!" My aunt then turned to my husband and me and asked, "What on earth is she talking about?"

We told Mom's sister and the rest of the family, "This is normal, and it's a good thing. Don't worry." We then shared with them information about the departing visions.

"She's talking to people we can't see, and calling this 'scenes,'" I said to my worried aunt. "The dying will revert to the language of their youth, and for Mom it's Polish. She's being visited by deceased relatives or friends and we need for you to continue translating for us so that we can know who it is she is talking to." This not only eased my aunt's concern, but also soothed her grief.

With the help of my aunt's translating we quickly learned that Mom was having a passionate conversation with my father-in-law. As Mom talked back and forth between us and Pop, we noticed she was using the Yiddish word *malpe*. Malpe means "monkey," and this was Mom's nickname for Pop. Though his visit seemed to be reducing her fear of dying, she was still letting him know she wasn't ready to go. Michael and I knew she was stubborn, but wondered what was really behind her reluctance to move on.

Like Mom, my father-in-law had been a nonbeliever. As a matter of fact, his views on death were even more depressing than Mom's. He would say to us, "When I die I'll make tasty food for worms!"

The day after Thanksgiving in 1996, my father-in-law, or "Da," as my boys called him, suffered a paralyzing stroke. The kids were extremely upset—especially my older son, Aaron, who was devoted to his bigger-than-life grandfather. After Pop's health improved, the two of them were back to clowning around. The only difference was, Aaron would ride in his Da's lap in a wheelchair as they made loops around Mom.

Pop had lived a rich, active, and adventurous life. He was born in France, and as a young man he found himself at a Communist rally one afternoon; he was then promptly asked by the French government to leave the country! This incident provided us as a family with a wealth of jokes at Pop's expense, and the boys knew the story by heart. Expulsion from the land of his youth turned out to be divine intervention, because this actually saved both he and my mother-in-law from the Nazi death camps. Immigrating to the United States, he then turned around, enlisted in the Army, and served as a military medic in Europe. After the war he traveled to the concentration camps and found surviving family, bringing them back to the states.

Intuitively, I knew his stroke would eventually be his physical downfall, but talking about dying, death, and spirituality with him was pointless. He was a serious agnostic who had never completely grieved over the death of his father in France. Often, when there is an early loss or unresolved grief, spirituality suffers. With this awareness, I knew better than to share my experiences about otherworldly visitations with either of my in-laws.

Those who are dying will take care of us to the very end. Our loved ones will put death on hold until after a holiday, anniversary, or birthday. This is extremely common, and my father-in-law was no exception. In spite of his "all we are is worm food" attitude about death, Pop planned his own exit: He waited until after Hanukkah to die, so that my sons were able to enjoy their holiday. He knew Hanukkah, with eight nights of presents, was his grandsons' favorite time of the year. Once the holiday passed Pop left us with one final cherished memory: Having a wicked sense of humor, he began his spirit journey on Friday the 13th!

The morning after Pop physically died my husband, Michael, walked into our downstairs sunroom to find his father sitting on our couch in his favorite spot. No longer confined to a wheelchair, he looked healthy and happy. Michael said, "I felt like he was there to let me know he was okay." My response was, "Worm food? Who's laughing now, Pop?" That afternoon I walked over to my father-in-law's place to pick up a few mementos for my boys. Walking through the hallway, I saw one of his friends, a short, gray-haired woman. She waved me over. She was very persistent, so I went and sat down next to her. Instead of telling me how sorry she was about Pop's passing, she said, "I've seen your father-in-law this morning. He was just walking through the halls." We both smiled at one another knowingly and then sat for a few moments in silence. She knew I believed her.

As powerful as these afterlife communications were, neither my husband nor I shared them with his mom. The skeptic in her wasn't ready for such information, and we knew we needed to respect this.

HEALING OLD WOUNDS AS DEATH NEARS

Six years later, we watched Mom call out to Pop by his Yiddish nickname, Malpe. Her conversations with him were now very lively, and the more she talked the more relaxed she became. She even seemed less anxious about leaving us and joining Pop in the afterlife. With my father-in-law's visitation the first step in healing old wounds had been taken. Any remaining fear of death she had was evaporating. At this point, all Michael and I could do was grin.

Meanwhile, as my in-laws' reunion continued, the hospice worker at the bedside was growing even more controlling, ordering an even stronger medication for Mom's "significant hallucinations." I could tell that underneath her pushy exterior she was downright frightened by what she was seeing.

My mother-in-law was not in pain, and she didn't need strong narcotics. Looking at her chatting away, we knew she was just fine. The hospice worker wanted Mom sedated because *she*—not

Mom—was uncomfortable with the departing visions. As a family we voted "No more medications," but the hospice worker still tried to make us feel guilty. I finally took her by the arm, escorted her out of the room, and said, "It's really okay. We can take it from here."

When I returned to Mom's room, I noticed her mood had changed, and she was no longer talking to Pop. Now speaking to someone else, her eyes were beginning to well up with tears. Suddenly, she cried out to her mother, who had been gassed to death in Auschwitz during the Holocaust. Listening quietly, we realized she was finally confronting the deep emotional grief she had carried for almost seven decades. After my mother-in-law and father-in-law escaped to the United States, Hitler's rage rained down hard upon all of Europe. Family left in Poland ended up in Siberia gulags or Nazi concentration camps. Carried to the camps in icy-cold cattle cars, the family barely survived. When the train finally stopped in Auschwitz, my mother-in-law's mother, brother, sister, brother-in-law, cousins, and friends were brutally pushed out of the cattle cars and into a scene of barbaric cruelty and chaos. The Nazis immediately began to divide families up. Younger people were separated from older family members, as were husbands from wives and children from parents. Mom's sister would not leave her mother's side and instead grabbed her hand more tightly. Her mother took in the panic and turmoil around her, and quickly understood what was happening: There was a line for camp workers and another for the gas chambers. She pushed her daughter into the line for the camp workers, knowing this would save her from certain death. A tall Nazi saw what she was doing and angrily shoved the mother into the death line. Saving her daughter cost my mother-in-law's mother her life. Living in the States Mom didn't know where her family was, and living with not knowing who was alive or dead for so many months had a devastating effect on her. Unresolved grief over the violent death of her mother and other family members in the camps was a wound that never healed.

Tears were running down our cheeks as Mom sat up in her bed and called out to her mother who had died so brutally. This loss, which had almost destroyed her with Survivor's Guilt and had been at the core of so much anguish, was finally dissolving before our eyes. Mother and daughter had found each other, and I was able to witness this. It truly was a grand reunion. The lifelong anguish that had been at the core of her fear of dying was suddenly no more. She was almost ready to go.

Mom was extremely lucid the rest of the day. When my husband, children, or I would speak to her, she would turn and talk to us. She knew we were in the room, and she told us she loved us. She also hugged her sister, nephews, and nieces. Being 88 years old, and having healed spiritually, she finally realized it was time for her to move on. The visitations from Pop and her mother helped her finally begin to let go. Death was nothing to fear.

A Departing Vision for Me

Later on that evening, the storm passed and Mom was finally sleeping peacefully. We were not sure when she would leave, but knew it would be soon. Acceptance had taken over and she was now ready to go with her mother and Pop. Turning to Mom I took her hand in mine and said, "You are safe. It's alright. I love you." Michael also added, "I love you, Mom. Tell Pop 'Hi' for me." After kissing her we made our way home to our boys and a hot cooked meal.

As we walked into the house Aaron and Joshua left their computer games, came downstairs, and asked how Grandma was doing. I told them, "She's almost ready to move to her new home." Growing up with a mother who openly investigated afterlife matters, they both knew what I was saying. After a few tears, dinner, and cups of hot chocolate we made our way to our beds, hoping to grab a few hours of sleep.

I'd just nodded off when suddenly I felt something shake me. I woke up and knew Mom had finally passed. Rubbing my eyes, I said out loud to her, "You had to wait 'til everyone left before you would go?" If the dying believe their death will upset us they will wait until they are alone before moving on. Looking at the clock I saw that it was 2:40 in the morning. Just down the street my mother-in-law had finally shed her tired body and was crossing the threshold separating this life from the next, escorted by my father-in-law and her mother.

Pushing warm quilts aside, I hugged my tired husband and told him we needed to call Mom's place. Picking up the phone, we quickly learned she had indeed begun her new journey at the exact moment I had awakened.

AFTERLIFE HUGS FROM MY OWN MOTHER

Waking up from a deep sleep knowing someone has died was nothing new for me. I had just turned 16 when my own mother, Carol, passed. At 5 in the morning I awoke and knew her spirit had finally escaped her cancer-ridden body. I was not the only one who felt my mother leave. My cousin Virginia Pilegard, also a well-published author, had this to share:

> Your Aunt Helen and I were both awakened on the morning of Carol's death. In a dream, I saw a figure in white I recognized to be Jesus standing by Carol's hospital bed and heard the words, "Everything is going to be alright." My mother called and said, "Something's happened with Carol." Carol was so ill by this time, I had little faith anything would ever be alright again. I had no understanding of what I had dreamed. "She died," my mom explained. Later someone called and confirmed your mother's death. I don't remember who.

Virginia told me she now believes her departing vision was telling her my mother was no longer in pain, but in a healing place. My mother's two best friends were also awakened early that morning, and my friend Richard Asadoorian told me both he and a nurse friend of the family felt my mother's spirit leave just as dawn broke. All five of us, living in separate locations, received one last hug from her as she left her earthly body and joined her parents and brother on the other side.

For years I didn't know my aunt, my cousin, or my mother's two friends had also been touched by her departure. No one in my family knew how to grieve or talk about life after death, so I tucked my otherworldly experience away and didn't share it with anyone until I was much older.

Years later, after hearing similar afterlife accounts from bereaved clients, I decided I'd try to find an explanation for these experiences. In London, I finally found my first answer in a musty old bookstore. Digging through a stack of old prints, a tattered book fell off the shelf and almost hit me in the head. It was titled *Deathbed Visions*. Written by physicist Sir William Barrett, it was published the year after his death in 1926. Barrett and his wife, Lady Florence Barrett, an obstetric surgeon, collected numerous accounts throughout the years. Here is one such story from their collection.

My father died on Thursday, December 30, 1869, in Kensington, England. When my brother returned from Australia a few years after that, he told us that one night, whilst camping out, he had gone to rest and had slept, and he awoke seeing my father's head distinctly in one part of the tent. It made such an impression on him that he went to his mate in the adjoining tent and said, "I have seen my father; you must come and stay with me." By the next mail he received a letter telling him of my father's death.

My brother said it must have been about 3 a.m. when he saw my father. Would not that correspond with our 3 p.m.? [Australia is about 11 hours ahead of the United Kingdom.] I always think they must have seen each other at the same time."[1]

Devouring the words in this book, I found myself spellbound. I then picked up another historical book on departing visions, *Death and Its Mystery: At the Moment of Death* by C. Flammarion, and read the following account:

It was during the war with Italy that, one day in June, 1859, a friend of mine was breaking his journey at Marseilles. He had stretched himself out on his bed at 6 o'clock in the evening, to rest from his travels. What was his stupefaction to see his brother, of whom he was extremely fond, pass across the room, when he knew he was in Italy, with the French expeditionary forces! He sprang out of bed and ran after him; but, alas! It was only a shade, which vanished as it had appeared.

Some weeks before this vision, he had received a letter from his brother, telling him that he was in good health, and that life in camp was a happy one (he was a volunteer).

When my friend went back to Corsica, his native land, about 20 days after this so-called vision, he found a letter from the Ministry of War awaiting him; it informed him that the young non-commissioned officer had died as a result of wounds received on the battlefield, on the day and at the time when the vision had occurred.

Finally, I was able to read in black and white print historical examples of departing visions similar to what I had experienced when my own mother passed. I was incredibly excited! At this same time, I was publishing self-help books on trauma, relationships, and healing. Feeling validated and exhilarated, I shared my newfound information on departing visions with my self-help-author friends. The response I typically received was, "Don't make too much of it. Sounds like just a coincidence. Remember, you were only 16 and probably traumatized."

I was definitely "traumatized" by the cancer that slowly consumed my mother for five years, but the departing vision I had after she passed left me feeling calm and relieved. Knowing my mother had survived her physical death helped me begin to heal.

Our Own Afterlife Shares Can Heal Those Around Us

By waking me up at 2:40 on the morning of her death, my mother-in-law, similar to my mother, Carol, had reassured me that life continued after physical death. One more departing soul took a moment to spiritually connect with me before traveling to the afterlife.

Knowing Mom was assisted in her passage from this earthly plane to the next by my father-in-law and her mother didn't eliminate our grief, but it did soften the pain. This also helped my boys, Aaron and Josh, heal from the loss they were feeling from their grandparent's passing.

Those who love us don't abandon us just because they leave this life. Consciousness survives, and contact continues. I believe my mother and my mother-in-law were still mothering me the moment they left their earthly remains behind. Similarly, in spite of physical death, my father-in-law continued to take care of my husband and sons.

I carry on by sharing my afterlife accounts with not only the bereaved, but with confused experiencers. Talking openly about my own otherworldly contacts is often more powerful than all of my professional grief resolution techniques combined. After sharing, I can see the stress, fear, and confusion melt away. Those I talk with eventually understand we don't die alone; death isn't frightening, and consciousness survives. Hope replaces distress, and healing begins.

CHAPTER 3

Using History to Heal

Death is only an experience through which you are meant to learn a great lesson: You cannot die.

—Paramahansa Yogananda, Indian yogi, guru, and author

WHY HISTORICAL ACCOUNTS ARE IMPORTANT

For decades I've been telling clients that as physical death approaches, departing visions can happen. If I'm working with someone whose loved one is getting ready to cross over, I share with them reports and accounts I've researched, experienced, or witnessed myself. Along with this, I can also show them examples of historical departing visions from countries around the globe. Learning that these experiences are universal gives grieving family and friends permission to begin letting go.

Why is this so important? We need to recognize that the physically dying will often stick around in order to take care of hurting family and friends, even if they are in great physical pain. But if a family can talk openly about physical death, the afterlife, and topics such as the departing vision, healing can begin. Such open discussion not only helps families, but also assists the dying in transitioning.

When family members can begin to let go, the physically dying will feel more emotionally comfortable in separating from their earthly bodies and making their way to the next dimension. It's imperative for surviving loved ones to know death isn't the end, and that holding on makes things harder for the dying. Historical and present-day departing vision accounts help me to achieve this task.

Maybe you've had a departing vision yourself, or witnessed someone you love talking to invisible visitors as death drew near. If so, you might be asking yourself, "What was this strange yet profound experience? Have other people had encounters like this? Am I the only one, and if not, why haven't I ever heard about such things?" As discussed in the previous chapters, departing visions are very common. In 1882, the Society for Psychical Research actually headed up one of the first studies to take a hard look at such visitations: 5,705 people were chosen at random and asked if they had ever encountered "phantasmal," ghostly, or spirit visions within the previous 12 years. The investigation concluded: "Between deaths and apparitions of the dying person a connection exists which is not due to chance alone."[1]

What did an early departing vision look like? In the late 1800s a British psychologist named Edmund Gurney (1847–1888) shared this account:

> On November 2nd and 3rd, 1870, I lost my two eldest boys, David Edward and Harry, from scarlet fever, they being then 3 and 4 years old respectively. Harry died at Abbot's Langley on November 2nd, 14 miles from my vicarage at Aspley, David the following day at Aspley. About an hour before the death of this latter child he sat up in bed, and pointing to the bottom of the bed said distinctly, "There is little Harry calling to me." Of the truth of this fact I am sure, and it was heard also by the nurse.
>
> [Signed] X.Z., Vicar of N[2]

Notice how the vicar who reported this departing vision decided not to share his name. Possibly he was fearful of ridicule. In 1886, another experience by Miss Berta Hurly, living in South Shropshire, England, had a similar encounter while having dinner with her family. Sadly, she was then laughed at after sharing what she saw!

> Waterbeach Vicarage, Cambridge, February, 1890.
>
> In the spring and summer of 1886 I often visited a poor woman called Evans, who lived in our parish,

Caynham. She was very ill with a painful disease, and it was, as she said, a great pleasure when I went to see her; and I frequently sat with her and read to her. Towards the middle of October she was evidently growing weaker, but there seemed no immediate danger. I had not called on her for several days, and one evening I was standing in the dining-room after dinner with the rest of the family, when I saw the figure of a woman dressed like Mrs. Evans, in large apron and muslin cap, pass across the room from one door to the other, where she disappeared.

I said, "Who is that?"

My mother said, "What do you mean?" and I said, "That woman who has just come in and walked over to the other door." They all laughed at me, and said I was dreaming, but I felt sure it was Mrs. Evans, and next morning we heard she was dead.

[Signed] Berta Hurly[3]

The family who had made fun of Berta during the evening meal eventually learned that Mrs. Ewans, who was at her home, had lost consciousness at the exact moment of her spirit appearance in the Hurly dining room. Ms. Hurly's mother acknowledged the following morning that the woman had passed.

"WIDE AWAKE" EXPERIENCES FROM HISTORY

One specific type of departing vision takes place when an experiencer is not dying, and is wide awake. While fully conscious, these experiencers are visited by departing loved ones. Souls moving on to the afterlife appear very real to those who see them. Along with this, the experiencers are often unaware a death is occurring or has just taken place. They may not even know the dying person has been ill or close to death. Because of this, the individual receiving the visitation is taken completely by surprise! Shortly after the visitation, the experiencer discovers that the person who appeared to them has just died in another location.

Andrew Lang (1844–1912), a Scottish poet, novelist, and literary critic, shared the following account in his 1899 work, *The Book of Dreams and Ghosts.*

In the month of November (1785 or 1786), Sir John Sherbrooke and Colonel Wynyard were sitting before dinner in their barrack room at Sydney Cove, in America. It was duskish, and a candle was placed on a table at a little distance. A figure dressed in plain clothes and a good round hat passed gently between the above people and the fire. While passing, Sir J. Sherbrooke exclaimed, "God bless my soul, who's that?"

Almost at the same moment Colonel W. said, "That's my brother John Wynyard, and I am sure he is dead." Colonel W. was much agitated, and cried and sobbed a great deal. Sir John said, "The

fellow has a devilish good hat; I wish I had it."
(Hats were not to be got there and theirs were worn
out.) They immediately got up (Sir John was on
crutches, having broken his leg), took a candle, and
went into the bedroom, into which the figure had
entered. They searched the bed and every corner of
the room to no effect; the windows were fastened
up with mortar.... They received no communication
from England for about five months, when a letter
from Mr. Rush, the surgeon (Coldstream Guards),
announced the death of John Wynyard at the moment, as near as could be ascertained, when the
figure appeared.[4]

In this 1785 account, several men in America are
visited by the spirit of a dying man in England. Notice
how quickly the man's brother recognizes this visitation as a sign that his beloved brother is beginning his
journey to the afterlife. During earlier times departing
visions were often accepted as messages from the beyond.
When experiencers had an encounter such as this, they
understood a physical death had occurred.

In the following 1867 account a visitation from a deceased daughter and sister prepares a mother and brother
for an upcoming passing.

In 1867, Miss G., aged 18, died suddenly of
cholera in St. Louis. In 1876, one of her brothers,
F.G., who was much attached to her, had done a
good day's business as a commercial traveler in St.
Joseph. He was sending in his orders to his employ-
ers and was smoking a cigar, when he became conscious that someone was sitting on his left, with one
arm on the table. It was his dead sister. He sprang

up to embrace her (for even on meeting a stranger whom we take for a dead friend, we don't realize the impossibility in the half-moment of surprise), but she was gone. Mr. G. stood there, the ink wet on his pen, the cigar lighted in his hand, the name of his sister on his lips. He had noted her expression, features, dress, the kindness of her eyes, the glow of her complexion, and something he had never seen before: a bright red scratch on the right side of her face.

Mr. G. took the next train home to St. Louis, and told the story to his parents. His father was inclined to ridicule him, but his mother nearly fainted. When she could control herself, she said that, unknown to anyone, she had accidentally scratched the face of the dead woman years ago, apparently with the pin of her brooch, while arranging something about the corpse. She had obliterated the scratch with powder, and had kept the fact to herself. "She told me she knew at least that I had seen my sister," Mr. G. said. A few weeks later Mrs. G. died.[5]

Did the deceased daughter make an appearance to prepare both Mrs. G. and her brother for the mother's upcoming passing?

If you've experienced a departing vision and have never told anyone about it, now you see you aren't alone. A century or so ago departing visions were more openly discussed, but actual accounts were often rejected by intellectuals and the scientific-minded. Today, most of the general population doesn't even know what these otherworldly visitations are. Not long ago I received the following departing vision inquiry from Italy. Here we have another experience looking for validation.

Five months ago my mother died from natural causes. A few days before this she confided in me that she had witnessed the appearance of a woman and had watched her for a few minutes. The second and third time she appeared was during the second and third day after this initial appearance.

The first two appearances were basically the same, but on the third, the woman extended her hand to my mother as if she were asking her to go with her. Mom died at dawn the next morning. She was only 64 years old. I think the woman who came to take her with her was her mother (my grandmother). Not a day goes by when I don't ask Mom to tell me if she is at least well and if she is with her mother.

Please confirm and help me, even if it's just to understand what science really thinks happens before death.

This experiencer contacted me because she was confused about what her mom had seen. She didn't have an expectation about what I was going to tell her and was even willing to hear a physiological, scientific explanation. She just wanted some answers. For me this isn't an unusual request. I was able to calm her concerns by sharing historical departing visions similar to those I have presented to you.

ASSISTING THE DYING AND
THEIR FAMILIES

I recently spent several days by a dying friend's bedside before he crossed over. With his family I openly discussed historical departing visions. As a result of this, his family members calmed down. Once the dying gentleman, an elderly Frenchman, saw that his family was more at peace, he was able to make a long-needed apology to his wife, owning up to infidelity in the relationship that had never been resolved. Furthermore, during World War II he had escaped the invasion of the Nazis, but was then captured and placed in a labor camp. In other words, my friend carried a lot of painful baggage with him throughout his life.

As physical death drew near, my friend began speaking to his family on the other side in French. It was obvious that the end of his physical suffering was right around the corner. At this same time, the words "I'm sorry," about his extramarital affair, escaped his parched lips. This brought both me and his wife to tears. With one foot in this life and the other in the next dimension, amends for a marital affair that had taken place so many years ago were finally being made. This apology tied up loose ends for the couple, relieving the surviving wife of resentments she had been carrying for 20 years. Once the man passed the wife was able to grieve more easily.

Is this an unusual deathbed scene? Absolutely not. Apologies such as this have been reported throughout history.

In my experience, sharing historical examples of the departing vision, along with research collected from individuals who have had these encounters, has proven to be very affirming for both the surviving family and those preparing to move on. The following are just a few of the accounts I often share when physical death is imminent.

CHRISTIANITY, JUDAISM, AND HISTORICAL DEPARTING VISIONS

The religion of Christianity is based on a strong belief in life after death. Jesus of Nazareth foretold many of the details of his arrest, trial, and death—*before* his crucifixion. The New Testament contains several versions of this. According to these writings, on three separate occasions Jesus made predictions about his eventual death, and each prophecy came true. He first tells his disciples he will be rejected by the elders and chief priests. He also informs his followers he will be killed. At the "Last Supper" in Jerusalem during Passover, he announces to his apostles that one of them will betray him by turning him over to the authorities. Finally, Jesus tells the apostle Peter he will deny knowing him later on that day. As we know, all of Jesus's premonitions leading up to his crucifixion on the cross come to pass. These powerful spiritual experiences molded much of Christianity.

Given that the story of Jesus's death is so well documented, why are departing visions not more accepted? In most religious Christian settings, the departing vision is unheard of. Worse, in some extreme fundamentalist sects, visions of the deceased are seen as "the devil's work." But the religious tradition of Christianity is rich in near-death experiences, after-death communications, and departing visions. Hopefully today's Christian experiencers and clergy will begin to come forward and openly discuss these subjects with their congregations.

If we think only Christianity has a difficult time supporting those who experience otherworldly visitations, we must think again: Within Jewish traditions as well, this topic is very hush-hush! Because of this, the majority of the general population is unaware that Judaism *accepts* the concept of an afterlife! As one recent Jewish writer wrote, "Judaism has absolutely always had a view of the afterlife. From the 14th century on, a belief in *gilgul*, or reincarnation, was as kosher as Manischewitz. ...there's a line in the bedtime Shema [prayer], 'Forgive anyone who has harmed me in this incarnation or any other incarnation.'"[6]

Recently, a Jewish friend of mine named Robin, who has witnessed several fantastic departing visions, sent me the following note:

> I attended the funeral of my 94-year-old aunt yesterday.... She wanted to die for years.... The rabbi (at the funeral) said, without room for misinterpretation, that after we die we are "dust in the wind"; we rest. No reference to a spirit with awareness or "afterlife" was mentioned. I really thought the Jewish religion abandoned that conception a long time ago.

I just love Robin! She's very comfortable with afterlife encounters, and when she needs help, she asks for it. In response to her note, I told her not only is the idea of an afterlife indeed part of modern-day Judaism, but also departing visions have been documented by rabbis for centuries.

In my first book on the departing visions of the dying, *One Last Hug Before I Go: The Mystery and Meaning of Deathbed Visions*, I gave examples from Rabbi Simcha Raphael's wonderful research in his work titled *Jewish Views of the Afterlife*. In reviewing Raphael's research, several accounts really caught my eye. He writes about the departing visions of two historical Hassidic rabbis, Rabbi Shmelke and Rabbi Zalman. Both of these well-known rabbis were famous sages and Kabbalists. Let's begin with Rabbi Shmelke. In 1861, this much-loved religious leader was dying. On his deathbed he received a visit from his deceased father-in-law and teacher. "In the hour before he died, Rabbi Shmelke of Sasov saw standing beside him his deceased father Rabbi Moshe Leib (1745–1807), and his great teacher, Rabbi Mikhal of Zlotchov."[7] Rabbi Shmelke's beloved father-in-law and his devoted teacher were both there to escort him from this life to the next.

Centuries before Hollywood mediums hit the television airwaves there were other famous rabbis who also reported departing visions. One such rabbi was the first Rabbi of Chabad, Schneur Zalman. The offspring of mystics, philosophers, and Kabbalists, he was a great force in Jewish history. As the founder of the world's largest branch of Chasidic or Orthodox Judaism known as *Chabad*, Zalman continues to be revered by Jews around the world today. In 1812, after living a very full life, Rebbe Zalman received a vision of the origins of creation: "Rabbi Schneur Zalman of Liadi, shortly before his death, turned to his grandson and asked, 'Do you see anything?' The boy looked at him in astonishment. Then the rabbi said, 'All I can see is the divine nothingness which gives life to the world.'"[8]

Unlike Christianity, these historical departing visions come from a religious tradition in which afterlife matters are rarely discussed. Thankfully, because of Rabbi Raphael's work, Judaism is again being infused with afterlife concepts. This in turn will give Jews permission to openly share their own departing visions, near-death experiences, or after-death communications.

ISLAMIC DEPARTING VISIONS

Christianity and Judaism aren't the only religions with a history of otherworldly visitations and encounters. Within the Islamic tradition, we also find powerful examples of the departing vision.

Muhammad ibn Abdullah (570–632), or the prophet Muhammad, was the founder of the Islamic faith. For Muslims around the world he is the prophet of God. Muhammad had encounters with the angel Gabriel for 23 years, and these visions are the foundation for the Muslim's holy text, the Quran or Koran. How did these angelic visitations occur?

While meditating in one of his favorite caves just outside Mecca, Muhammad, who was in his early 40s, was reflecting on the discord and tribal upheaval he was seeing in his community. He was very troubled by this. As he sat silently in reflection, the angel Gabriel suddenly appeared to him, hugged him tightly, and then asked him to repeat a series of words. After a very surprised Muhammad did as he was asked, the angel disappeared. Feeling overwhelmed, the frightened prophet left the cave. Making his way down the hill he heard a voice say to him, "Oh, Muhammad, you are the Messenger of God and I am Gabriel."[9]

Once back in his village Muhammad then shared with his wife and followers what the angel Gabriel had said to him. The story truly amazed everyone. Three years after this extraordinary encounter Muhammad began preaching publicly to all who would listen, "God is one!"

The Islamic prophet's visions of Gabriel continued throughout his life until his death at the age of 62 in 632 CE. During one of his last few encounters with the angel Gabriel, Muhammad learned about his own upcoming death, and that of his beloved daughter. Muhammad's daughter by his first wife Khadijah was named Fatima. She was told about the premonition her father had about both his death and hers. After his death, she shared her father's secret departing vision with her mother Khadijah, who had this to say: "The Prophet said, 'Every year Gabriel used to revise the Quran with me once only, but this year he has done so twice. I think this portends my death, and you will be the first of my family to follow me.'"[10] The Prophet Muhammad's daughter Fatima died six years after he passed.

Not only did this prophet have incredible departing visions, but throughout history many of his followers have also reported seeing him as their own physical death draws near. Visitations from Muhammad continue to this day, and are considered a common and blessed occurrence. Folowing is a modern-day account.

In 1998 the Arab world's best-known television preacher of the Holy Quran died. In 2002 during the holy Muslim celebration of Ramadan, a special Egyptian television program reported that the popular Egyptian preacher had been visited by the Prophet Muhammad as he lay dying on his deathbed, and greeted him out loud while repeating the Islamic testimony of faith.[11]

Premonitions of physical death can be found in most religious traditions. The accounts I've included are just a few examples of how prevalent these experiences are in our world religions. Regardless of the particular spiritual philosophy, the departing visions tend to be very similar. Common characteristics, such as seeing deceased loved ones or religious entities, receiving premonitions of an upcoming passing, and having visions of the afterlife, can be easily identified. The founders of these spiritual movements spoke openly about such encounters centuries ago. In light of this, why do so many modern-day religious leaders continue to dismiss the departing vision? Those of us who follow a particular spiritual tradition would benefit greatly from the open discussion with our clergy of historical departing visions.

The physically dying who have had afterlife encounters often tell me, "I've discovered all religions lead to the same place! No one religion is the only religion! I wish I could tell my priest/minister/rabbi/imam/pastor about this." Such awareness brings both the grieving and dying a great sense of peace, but can create difficulty for unaware clergy.

Religious leaders must become willing to acknowledge the departing visions tucked away in the pages of historical doctrine. Along with this they need to recognize that some members of their congregations have had afterlife encounters. Exploring modern-day departing visions will also aid the physically dying, terminally ill, and grieving. Such openness can only benefit any house of worship.

Famous Departing Visions

Aside from sharing religious departing visitations, I love enlightening people with the otherworldly premonitions experienced by well-known individuals. These reports give everyday experiencers permission to embrace their own departing visions. Without further ado, here are several accounts from some very famous people.

A Pope Is Visited

The controversial Alexander VI (1431–1503) was the pope from 1492 until his death in 1503. His birth name was Roderic Llançol I Borja, and he was quite the character. Borja lived the wild life before and while he was pope. Aside from having a family previous to becoming the most powerful religious leader of his time, he had a number of very colorful mistresses while in the papacy. Murder, thievery, obscene banquets, prostitution, drunkenness, incest, and rape were all part of his legacy. Because the Borja family had such an interesting history, Hollywood turned the murdering dynasty into a television series. Called *The Borgias*, the program has popularized the debauchery and criminal activity recorded in the lives of Alexander VI and his dysfunctional family.

As was his life, death for this pope was also full of drama. Borja became ill with fever after dining with one of his cardinals. The theory is, he was poisoned. One would think such a villain would never make it to the afterlife, but his last words have been reported as, "Okay, okay, I'll come. Just give it a moment." ("Va bene, va bene, arrivo. Aspettate un momento.")[12] Who was he talking to? Was he being visited by deceased relatives, friends, or perhaps a forgiving mistress from the other side? We will never know.

A Beloved Composer Has a Departing Vision

Can you imagine composing a musical piece on your deathbed? This is just what Johann Sebastian Bach (1685–1750) did. His classical works are played at most of the weddings I attend, but what gave him the spiritual strength to compose as he lay dying? Blind, suffering respiratory complications, and afflicted with several strokes, this beloved musical genius was somehow able to compose on his deathbed, "Before Thy Throne I Now Approach." He was able to finish it because, during the hours just before his passing, he supposedly regained his vision. Another theory is that he was "seeing the unseen as often occurs in the last days of life."[13]

An Extraordinary Presidential Departing Vision

John Adams (1735–1826) was a leading supporter and defender of America's independence from Britain in 1776. He was also the sixth president of the United States. He died on the Fourth of July in 1826. On the day of his passing, as he lay on his deathbed, he said, "Oh, yes; it is the glorious Fourth of July. It is a great day. It is a good day. God bless it. God bless you all."[14] He then lapsed into unconsciousness. Later, he awoke and mumbled, "Thomas Jefferson still survives!"[15] After this, Adams left this life for the world to come.

As he was preparing to leave his physical body behind, there is no way he would have known about Jefferson's death. His onetime political rival and good friend passed in a different location, just a few hours earlier, on that same Fourth of July day in 1826. While Adams was dying did his good friend Jefferson come for him?

One final note on Adams and Jefferson: Both of these men defended our freedoms and were among our first presidents. I find it interesting that they both left this life for the afterlife within hours of each other on the same day, exactly 50 years after the signing of the Declaration of Independence.

A Gifted Pianist Loses His Fear of Death

Frederic François Chopin (1810–1849), the famous Polish composer and extraordinary classical pianist is often referred to as the "Poet of the Piano," but how many of us know he was terrified of being buried alive?

The gifted musician was ill for many years, and death seemed always to be just around the corner. When his passing was imminent, Chopin's sister rushed to his bedside. Just after midnight on October 17, 1849, the composer awoke from a deep sleep. His physician then leaned over him and asked if he was suffering or in pain. Chopin replied, "Not anymore."[16] After struggling for years with an overwhelming fear of death, the famous pianist finally died in the arms of his loving sister. He was only 39 years old.

How did this composer who worried incessantly about being buried alive somehow come to terms with his passing? Maybe he had a departing vision or caught a quick look at what life without a physical body would be like. Was it this sense of reassurance that relieved him of his pain and allowed him to move on to the great celestial orchestra in the sky?

At Chopin's request, his heart was preserved in alcohol after his death and has been kept in his homeland in a sealed jar inside a pillar at Warsaw's Holy Cross Church. The pillar was dedicated to Chopin, and when I last visited this church I noticed that flowers continue to be placed here in honor of the musician.

Premonitions of an Infamous Death

The handsome and charismatic John Fitzgerald Kennedy (1917–1963) was the 35th president of the United States. Easy on the eyes and a political force to be reckoned with, he was the youngest man ever elected to that office. The dashing and controversial Kennedy was also the youngest president to ever to die in office. On November 22, 1963, an assassin's bullets killed him as his motorcade made its way through the streets of Dallas, Texas.

Almost everyone knows that story. But most people don't know that the young president had a departing vision. On his arrival in Dallas he said to special assistant Arthur M. Schlesinger Jr., "If someone is going to kill me, they will kill me."[17]

What a powerful, prophetic statement. President Kennedy had this premonition just hours before his violent assassination.

The Prime Minister of India Has a Spiritual Forewarning

Indira Gandhi (1917–1984) was an incredibly strong and dominant figure in India for almost two decades. She was also prime minister on four different occasions. A political genius, Gandhi started a family planning program, addressed food shortages, and authorized the development of nuclear weapons in 1967. Sadly, this little powerhouse of a woman was assassinated by her own bodyguards. Sikh militants fired 33 bullets into her chest and abdomen, killing her at her own residence.

The night before her assassination Indira Gandhi said the following: "I don't mind if my life goes in the service of the nation. If I die today every drop of my blood will invigorate the nation."[18]

ANOTHER GREAT EQUALIZER

It has often been said that death is the great equalizer: No matter the size of our bank account or our position in society, all of us are going to eventually die the physical death. Sadly, our culture does little to prepare us for this great event. Many medical personnel, mental healthcare providers, educators, and clergy are death-phobic, so they are of little help.

Thankfully, the departing vision is also a great equalizer. Examples of this spiritual event have been documented throughout history and can be found in all major religions. Visitations from deceased loved ones, angels, or religious icons occur in all cultures, and these experiences are incredibly similar to one another. Whether it's a U.S. president born in the 1700s, an 18th-century

Jewish religious leader, a politician in India born in the early 1900s, or my dear friend who passed just a year ago, a deceased loved one is always there to gently escort us to the afterlife.

A PERSONAL GOODBYE

Understanding the nature of the departing vision definitely lessens grief. As I finish writing this chapter, a relative of mine has just physically died in England. Due to a series of very unfortunate events, he had been seriously ill for the last few years. Several days ago he decided enough was enough, and this dear man stopped eating and drinking. He then began having fantastic departing visions.

His wife made her way to the afterlife shortly after his illness set in. The feisty blond with the thick northern accent was his soul mate, and was loved by all. During her visits to the States she would lather herself in suntan lotion and "bake" for hours in a lounge chair. This British cousin loved our sunshine. When she died suddenly, her husband was devastated. We didn't know if he would survive the loss. For a short period of time he remained, but soon it was time for him to go too.

As this relative prepared to pass he had visions of his devoted wife. She had come to escort him to the other side. The family wasn't frightened by these visitations; they were comforted when he called out to her. After he escaped his paralyzed body, we as a family knew husband and wife had a glorious reunion. May peace be with you two. Be sure to stop by Disneyland before you take off for the heavens. Someday we will meet again.

CHAPTER 4

Scientific Research: The Early Days

Frisbeetarianism is the belief that when you die, your soul goes up on the roof and gets stuck.
—George Carlin

George Carlin was a brilliant American comic who tackled taboo subjects in his stand-up acts. One such routine looked at how we as a society deal with death and dying. Dressed in black, he poked fun at our denial and fears, all while standing on a stage littered with tombstones. I saw the show live and thought I'd never stop laughing. Using humor, Carlin did what most in our culture refuse to do: He addressed death phobia head-on. Sadly, our society continues to suffer from a great deal of death phobia. This overwhelming fear leaves many of us totally unprepared for any form of an afterlife encounter.

The general public is unaware that the departing vision has a long history of scientific investigation, dating back several centuries. Societal death phobia has kept this fact hidden away. If death is inevitable, and departing visions are common, why are most of us unacquainted with this phenomenon? Wouldn't such information take the sting out of dying and free us up to focus more on living?

We can begin to remedy this by following in George Carlin's footsteps. Let's take a look at a few early departing-vision investigations.

Groundbreaking Investigators

We have already talked about the Society for Psychical Research and its early investigations into the departing vision. Also known as the SPR, the organization was founded in Britain in 1882. The prestigious membership consisted of well-respected professors, physicists, scientists, doctors, and psychiatrists, all of whom utilized scientific research methods in their investigations. One top priority was to scientifically research those phenomena and experiences that supported the case for life after death. In spite of their many findings, they continually received condemnation from the more established scientific community. Centuries later, not much has changed!

A CENSUS OF HALLUCINATIONS

Not long ago, with the lack of medical care and understanding of disease, death was very prevalent. When death is part of the everyday landscape of life, phobic reactions are less common. With earlier societies, news related to dying and death was included in everyday, regular conversation. There was no tip-toeing around the topic. Because of this, departing visions were more readily accepted by many members of the general population. This assumption was even tested in 1889 with a survey, which was one of the very first departing-vision studies.

In that year Henry Sidgwick (1838–1900), a philosopher, economist, and one of the founders and first presidents of the SPR, decided to collect a "Census of Hallucinations." This five-year survey looked at the hallucinatory experiences of the general population. Those who responded were required to be in good health, and had been awake if and when an event occurred.

Sidgwick, along with his team of researchers, asked the question, "Have you ever, when believing yourself to be completely awake, had a vivid impression of seeing or being touched by a living being or inanimate object, or of hearing a voice; which impression, so far as you could discover, was not due to any external physical cause?"[1] The researchers received 17,000 replies, of which almost 10 percent answered in the affirmative.

In analyzing the responses the research team was surprised to discover many examples of what they termed "crisis apparitions" or "death coincidence." They discovered the reported apparitions were actually visions of individuals either having a dramatic crisis or dying.

These visions occurred when the interviewed person was wide awake, shortly before, during, or after the actual event witnessed. The experiencer was also in a location away from where the crisis or death was taking place. The visions occurred within 12 hours of the dying experience—again, whether before, during, or after the death.

In taking on such a controversial study, Sidgwick and his team risked their credibility. Their groundbreaking investigation set the stage for future research, as their courage and commitment provided me and other investigators with a legacy to build upon.

SIR WILLIAM BARRETT

At the time of the Census on Hallucination, other researchers were also busily gathering departing visions. As I mentioned, the first book I ever read on these encounters was titled, *Deathbed Visions: The Physical Experiences of the Dying*, by Sir William Barrett, published in 1926, a year after the author's physical death. The original term used for the departing-vision experience was "deathbed vision."

Sir William Barrett (1844–1925) was born in Jamaica, British West Indies, and moved to England as a young person. He taught for 37 years as a professor of physics at the Royal College of Science in Dublin, and was knighted for his contributions to science in 1912. As we see, his groundbreaking book on the departing vision came after a long and illustrious career as a scientist, inventor, educator, and lecturer.

In his research into the deathbed or departing vision, Barrett's most treasured colleague was his wife, Lady

Florence Barrett, a prominent obstetric surgeon. I believe her afterlife encounters with her patients contributed to his interest in those departing visions reported by healthcare workers. Lady Barrett observed and recorded the departing visions she encountered with the women patients she worked with. Similar to most healthcare workers of her time, such experiences before a passing were not seen as unusual. Her patients would report visitations from deceased relatives, visions of the afterlife, and encounters with angels. Family at the bedside also reported seeing otherworldly escorts who had come to help their physically dying loved ones journey to the next life.

Along with collecting their own firsthand accounts, the Barretts began investigating the departing visions of other like-minded individuals. One such woman was a nurse named Joy Snell. Following is one of her first accounts, taken from her book, *The Ministry of Angels Here and Beyond*, first published in 1918.

> I awoke one night out of a sound sleep to find the room filled with light, although there was no light burning in it, and standing by my bedside was my dearest girl friend, Maggie. Addressing me by name she said: "I have a secret to tell you. I know that I am going over to the other world before long and I want you to be with me at the last and help to comfort my mother when I am gone."
>
> Before I had sufficiently recovered from my fear and amazement...she vanished, and the light slowly faded from the room....

A week later I was summoned to my friend's home. I found her suffering from a feverish cold, but there was...no presentiment of impending death.

Maggie's mother was called away...she asked me to stay with her daughter while she was absent.

One night, she was suddenly taken very ill. She expired in my arms....

It was the first death that I had witnessed. Immediately after her heart had ceased to beat, I distinctly saw something in appearance like smoke, or steam as it rises from a kettle in which the water is boiling, ascend from her body. This emanation rose only a little distance and there resolved itself into a form like that of my friend who had just died.... The face was that of my friend but glorified, with no trace upon it of the spasm of pain which had seized her just before she died.

After I became a professional nurse, a vocation which I followed for some 20 years, I witnessed scores of deaths. And always, immediately afterwards, I saw the spirit form, in appearance an etherialized duplicate of the human form, take shape above the body...and then vanish from my sight.[2]

Similar to the Barretts, Mrs. Snell was instrumental in systematically documenting numerous experiences she personally encountered and witnessed. To this day I use her tea kettle analogy, with the escaping steam representing the soul, when talking about dying, death, and the afterlife with clients, especially children.

Before his passing, physicist William Barrett gave a private lecture on afterlife survival to members of the SPR. On June 17, 1924, he made three points clear to the group: "I am personally convinced that the evidence we have published decidedly demonstrates (1) the existence of a spiritual world, (2) survival after death, and (3) of occasional communication from those who have passed over.... It is, however, hardly possible to convey to others who have not had a similar experience an adequate idea of the strength and cumulative force of the evidence that has compelled [my] belief."[3]

Barrett knew there would be those who would find his extensive research to be without merit, but he persevered until the end of his physical life. Though there are many departing visions from the Barrett collection, my all time favorite has to be this next one.

> Miss R. Canton, of Garway Road, London, W., sends me the following case, which I quote in her own words, as follows: "Some years ago I went to see a cousin of mine at Acton, who was very ill, and I was told by her sister that on the previous evening as she sat down on a chair by the bedside, the invalid exclaimed, 'Oh, don't! Oh, you have sent Mother away; she was sitting there!' and she continued to seem much distressed. My aunt had died some years previously. The dying girl told me about this herself when we were alone."[4]

A number of years ago, I was contacted by a woman who had witnessed a similar departing vision: A dying man was visited by a deceased relative, and during the visitation he became upset with his family at the bedside because they wouldn't get the deceased soul something to drink! Even as he made preparations to journey from this life to the next, being a good host was still important to him. Though a hundred years separate this account from Barrett's, the similarities are amazing.

CONSISTENT THEMES

Aside from collecting many incredible accounts, the Barretts discovered that regardless of the medical or situational differences between experiencers, the departing visions were undeniably similar. Here are just a few of the common themes they identified.

- ❂ At the moment of death or as a passing draws near the dying will receive visitations from relatives or friends they know are deceased.

- ❂ Persons preparing to die can also receive visitations from people who have recently passed on, even though they are unaware a death has occurred.

- ❂ Visitations from the deceased are often greeted by the dying with surprise, peace, and joy.

- ❂ Children who are dying and visited by angels are surprised to see that these angelic creatures do not have wings.

- ❂ Many of those who have departing visions are anxious to join their deceased loved ones on the other side.

- ❂ Dying becomes easier when departing visions occur.

As I mentioned earlier, William Barrett's tattered little green book let me know I wasn't crazy. Since then, it has been my goal to pass on to you this same sense of reassurance.

But I wasn't the only investigator touched by Sir and Lady Barrett. Though they were trailblazers, the Barretts' theories about the departing vision would be tested again, several decades later.

ENTER DRS. OSIS AND HARALDSSON

Psychologist Dr. Karlis Osis (1917–1997), born in Riga, Latvia, graduated from the University of Munich, and then worked as a research associate at Duke University. Osis was also the research director of the American branch of the SPR (Started by the famous American psychologist William James in 1884), and eventually became the group's senior researcher.

In the 1960s Osis decided to do a pilot study on deathbed or departing visions. He essentially confirmed what the Barretts had discovered in the late 1800s and early 1900s, and these results piqued his interests even more. Osis then teamed up with psychologist Erlendur Haraldsson to further investigate the visions of the dying.

Haraldsson is a professor emeritus of psychology at the faculty of social science at the University of Iceland. Born in Reykjavik, Iceland, in 1931, he studied philosophy at the universities of Iceland, Edinburgh, and Freiburg. The Icelander then went on to obtain a PhD from the University of Munich. Haraldsson was also a research associate at the American branch of the SPR.

Osis and Haraldsson conducted major cross-cultural surveys on the deathbed observations made by thousands of physicians and nurses in the United States and India. I received a copy of the original study from Dr. Haraldsson a number of years ago, but I'm going to simplify matters by sharing only the basic findings of the studies carried out between 1959 and 1973.

- ✪ Of the tens of thousands of dying patients studied, around 50 percent reported visions of some sort.

- ✪ These visions could involve deceased loved ones, other individuals, or mythical or religious figures.

- ✪ The purpose of such visitations was to escort the dying from this world to the afterlife.

- ✪ Dying persons often reported these "take away" escorts as unusual light or energy.

- ✪ Deathbed-vision reports depicted scenes of the "afterworld," with "luminous gardens," "buildings of great architectural beauty," and "symbolic transitional structures such as doors, gates, bridges," and rivers or boats.

- ✪ The afterlife was described as being populated with angelic beings that were glowing or brightly colored.

- ✪ There was a sense of unity with God or creation.

✪ Three quarters of those studied died within 10 minutes of their visions, whereas others passed on a few hours later.

Detailed specifics of these incredible investigations can be found in the researchers' 1977 book, *At the Hour of Death: A New Look at Evidence for Life After Death.* The Osis and Haraldsson studies found many of the same findings documented in earlier departing-vision research. One of my favorite Osis and Haraldsson accounts is the following.

A female cardiac patient in her 50s knew that she was dying and was in a discouraged, depressed mood. Suddenly, she raised her arms, and her eyes opened wide; her face lit up as if she was seeing someone she hadn't seen for a long time. She said, "Oh, Katie, Katie." The patient had been suddenly roused from a comatose state; she seemed happy, and she died immediately after the hallucination. There were several Katies in this woman's family: a half-sister, an aunt, and a friend. All were deceased.[5]

I love this particular afterlife experience because it depicts a dying woman who, previous to her departing vision with "Katie," was very depressed about her situation. After the visitation she made an about-face, and was joyous and ready to go!

Years ago a client told me how his father, after being in a comatose state, had a similar experience. As the family sat by the bedside, the once-nonresponsive gentleman suddenly became lucid, looked up toward the ceiling of the hospital room, raised his arms, and, with a delightful smile on his face, called out to his deceased wife. Within minutes after this he died peacefully. Once again we see just how similar departing visions are from one person to the next.

Here is one more account from the Osis and Haraldsson collection.

> A 70-year-old patient had seen her deceased husband several times, and then she predicted her own death. She said that her husband had appeared in the window and motioned to her to come out of the house. The reason for his visits was to have her join him. Her daughter and other relatives were present when she predicted her death and laid out her burial clothes. She laid down in bed for a nap and died about an hour later. She seemed calm, resigned to death, and, in fact, wanted to die. Before she saw her husband she didn't speak about imminent death. Her doctor was so surprised by her sudden death, for which there was no sufficient medical reason, that he checked to see if she had poisoned herself. He found neither signs of poisoning nor any such drugs in the house.[6]

Again, we have another wonderful example of a complete, unexpected mood change after having a departing vision.

ON BROAD SHOULDERS WE STAND

The Osis and Haraldsson cross-cultural studies with nurses and doctors opened the door wider for modern-day researchers. Those of us who have followed in their footsteps understand just how difficult research of this magnitude must have been. Since those early days, Osis and Haraldsson have been cited in hundreds of studies, books, and articles. Both men will forever be considered the godfathers of such research.

I feel especially blessed to still be regularly communicating with Dr. Haraldsson. My literary agent, John White, also a longtime afterlife investigator, edited Osis and Haraldsson's groundbreaking book *At the Hour of Death: A New Look at Evidence for Life After Death*. I truly have been a witness to history and stand on the broad shoulders of incredible researchers.

CHAPTER 5

Modern-Day Research Rebels

Everything science has taught me—and continues to teach me—strengthens my belief in the continuity of our spiritual existence after death. Nothing disappears without a trace.

—Wernher von Braun

As we have seen, not all scientists avoid life-after-death investigations; there are those few researchers who are bound and determined to go where their peers refuse to go! Many of these courageous explorers dedicate their lives to scientifically dissecting the mystery of life after death. In the last chapter we learned that the psychologist Dr. Osis was one of the premier researchers in the field. On December 26, 1997, he joined his own departed loved ones in the afterlife. This date also happened to be his 80th birthday.

His research partner, Dr. Haraldsson, is supposedly retired, but hasn't slowed down one bit. Still very active and now in his 80s, he continues to research not only departing visions, but also other topics involving survival after death, such as the spiritual visions and encounters of children.

Haraldsson is always respectful and supportive of other investigators, and not long ago he sent me findings based on his most recent afterlife research. His results are the product of a comprehensive Icelandic study on afterlife contact, and he has graciously given me permission to share some of his findings with you. For our purposes, I'm presenting only a brief account of Dr. Haraldsson's research.

An Icelandic Study from a World-Renowned Investigator

A national representative survey (902 respondents) conducted by the author indicated that 31 percent of the population in Iceland have had experiences of contact with persons who have died. A few years later the European Human Value survey, which was conducted in most West-European countries, showed that 25 percent of Europeans had been in contact with someone who had died....

The author and his associates conducted interviews with a large number of persons (around 450) who reported these experiences…which were interpreted as contacts with or apparitions of the dead. First they were asked to describe their experience and then many questions followed about the nature of the experience, circumstances in which the deceased person was, along with how and when he or she had died….

Most of these encounters or apparitions were with deceased relatives or loved ones, for example every second widow or widower had experienced their deceased spouse….[1]

For more information on this brilliant study, I encourage you to pick up a copy of Haraldsson's wonderful new book, titled, *The Departed Among the Living: An Investigative Study of Afterlife Encounters* (2012).

RELATIVE CONTACT

Haraldsson's particular point about widows and widowers has validated what I know to be true, both clinically and personally. For example, years ago I was visiting one of my relatives. His mother (my great aunt) and his wife had both passed. What he had to tell me was very surprising.

More than 10 years ago my great aunt received an after-death communication from my deceased grandfather, right before his funeral. After my grandfather contacted her, she told me she was concerned about the cemetery plot he was to be buried in. We had thought his remains would rest next to my grandmother's burial plot, but now there was some doubt. After making the drive, I found myself wandering around the family graveyard at dusk with nothing but a small flashlight.

After tripping over a few of my ancestors' tombstones, I finally found my grandmother's grave. Indeed, no earth had been turned near it for my grandfather's remains. After I returned from my cemetery reconnaissance mission, my great aunt told me she'd in fact been fearful the grave had yet to be dug. I was amazed at how right she had been. A decade later I learned that my grandfather's tired body had been cremated shortly after his death.

A few years later, both my great aunt and her son's wife passed away. During a visit to my cousin who had experienced these losses, I told him about my great aunt's after-death communication with my grandfather. Then I asked, "Since your wife passed, have you had contact with her?" Smiling, he replied, "Yes. I've seen her around the house a few times." He added that when he did see her she always looked healthy and well.

My cousin was never one for reading books on the survival of the soul after death, so his response wasn't what I would have expected. As he continued to talk about his visitations with his deceased wife, I could tell that these after-death communications brought him great comfort. My cousin believes his wife is not only watching over him, but is also waiting for him to join her.

Based on my own work, I've always suspected the statistics for after-death contact between surviving widows or widowers and their departed spouses was high, but Haraldsson's numbers surprised me! According to his results, half of this population appears to be having contact with deceased husbands, wives, and partners. The medical community might be wise to use such information to comfort the dying.

With more attention devoted to end-of-life care and hospice, the departing vision is becoming increasingly difficult to ignore. Thankfully there are medical professionals who have taken notice of these precious spiritual experiences. I call these modern-day investigators "rebels" because they are willing to defy their peers and risk ridicule by following in the footsteps of Barrett, Osis, and Haraldsson. With their research and studies they challenge not only the status quo, but their professional institutions as well.

The following modern-day research projects are a good example of this trend. Take a look at these scientific investigations. One comes to us from Italy, and one from Ireland.

AN ITALIAN INVESTIGATION

From Italy we learn of Paola Giovetti's research. Based on her investigations she states that 40 percent of those from her study experienced "take-away" or departing visions. Again, we have an incredible number of dying people reporting these experiences.

The following is just one account from her collection, in which a wife at the bedside learns her deceased mother is there to greet her husband who is about to pass.

> "The gauze over his face moved; I ran to him, and with his last strength he said to me, 'Adrianna, my dear, your mother [who had died three years before] is helping me break out of this disgusting body. There is so much light here, so much peace.'"[2]

Many men run from their wives' mothers, but not this one! After his vision he was frantic to leave his physically ill body and make his way to the other side! How comforting this must have been for his surviving wife.

IRISH SCHOLARS' ACCOUNTS

Ireland has a long history of interest in life after death. Reccurring mention of the afterlife can be found in songs, stories, and poetry. So it isn't surprising that one of the first actual documented accounts of an afterlife vision involves a 10th-century Irish scholar.

> Adamnan was a renowned scholar-abbot of Iona who traveled to the spiritual world and visited heaven, a purifying realm.... The vision of Adamnan describes a journey of Adamnan's soul, which is guided by an angel. He first travels through a fragrance-filled realm.... Historically, this account is very important because it is one of the first medieval Irish out-of-body experiences to be recorded.[3]

Unlike the historical Irish afterlife references found in myth and song, this is an authentic account from a true experiencer. Fast-forward a number of centuries and we discover science is now looking into Irish departing visions. These investigations had their start in England with Dr. Peter Fenwick. A neuropsychiatrist and neurophysiologist who has studied both epilepsy and end-of-life phenomena, Fenwick laid the necessary foundation for departing-vision researchers in the land of shamrocks. Here is one of his accounts.

The notion of death as the start of a journey is difficult to sustain since development of Western science, with the concept of consciousness as something that emerges from the brain, and therefore ends with brain death. However, the dying do not always experience the approach to death this way, and anecdotal accounts tell a different story often suggesting a continuation of a Journey after death. So it is essential to ask the dying what they experience as death approaches....

When we [Fenwick and colleagues] started this project in 2002, very little information was available on the mental states of the dying and very few studies had been published on end-of-life experiences. (Barrett 1926, Osis and Haraldsson 1986.) These end-of-life experiences we defined as a set of phenomena which occur in the last few days/weeks of life and are associated with the dying process. At the beginning of the study, we were interested in premonitions of dying, deathbed visions, transiting to new realities, terminal lucidity, and phenomena which occur at and just after death itself; e.g., deathbed coincidences, shapes or light seen surrounding or leaving the body. We were uncertain whether these phenomena truly occurred today, whether they were part of folklore, or whether, if they did occur, they could be attributed solely to medication or to the organic process of death itself.[4]

For this study, Fenwick and colleagues put together a scientific questionnaire on the mental states of the dying. This tool also explored experiences such as the departing vision. The questionnaire was then given to healthcare workers at two hospice facilities and one nursing home in England, along with two more nursing homes in the Netherlands. It was then used in an independent study in Ireland conducted by Una McConville and Regina McQuillan.

MacConville and McQuillan took the questionnaire developed by Fenwick and colleagues and had members of the Irish Association of Palliative Care document their experiences. After reviewing the collected material the researchers discovered this: Regardless of illness, cause of physical death, or medications used during treatment, the reported deathbed visions paralleled one another. Similar to Fenwick, Barrett, Osis, and Haraldsson, MacConville and McQuillan found that the medical professionals in their study witnessed patients encountering deceased relatives, white light, angels or religious figures, and the smell of roses.

Irish Times news reporter Fionala Meredith wrote a captivating story on this investigation in 2011, titled "Going into the Light." She shared what one of the nurses who participated in the study had to say: "I have often heard patients refer to seeing someone in their room or at the end of their bed, often relatives, and also it is not a distressing event for them."[5]

The nurse added that family members were often surprised and at times frightened by these visions. In working with the bereaved I have found this to be true, and I believe this particular point says a great deal about our society: Because we don't educate about the departing vision, some family members do become extremely overwhelmed when they occur. As opposed to using these experiences to begin the grieving process, opening up the discussion of physical death and the transition from this life to the next, many professional caregivers resort to medical or psychological excuses for departing-vision events. MacConville and McQuillan suggested that palliative-care professions needed more education about the nature of the departing vision. I agree with this, but would take it a step further: *All* medical personnel, mental healthcare providers, and clergy could benefit from such training. This would ease confusion and concern not only for family members, but also for the physically dying.

Meredith's story discussed another aspect of the dying process that continues to confound skeptics. Researchers MacConville and McQuillan found that 31 percent of those interviewed for this study reported they had encountered unconscious patients who would suddenly come to or wake up, right before dying.[6] After speaking lucidly and with a sense of calm with those at the bedside, they would gently pass. Here is what one respondent had to say about a dying patient who had emerged from a coma: "...the patient said he saw a light, a bright light; he died shortly afterwards."[7]

If the afterlife encounters of the physically dying were common topics of discussion in our everyday living experience, then the onset or sharing of such events would not be so startling.

MacConville and McQuillan validated another point I've been making for decades: The nature of the departing vision is radically different from a hallucination or drug-induced delusion. Being a seasoned mental healthcare professional, I've seen my fair share of clients who were suffering from hallucinations due to a number of mental health issues. The hallucination experiences I've encountered clinically are nothing like the departing vision. In assisting individuals suffering from alcohol or drug dependency for more than 30 years I have yet to encounter a state of intoxication even similar to the departing vision. I also believe that medications used for pain management are not responsible for departing vision events, and MacConville and McQuillan also found this to be true, reporting that 68 percent of those who responded to the questionnaire agreed that departing visions differed from hallucinations.[8] MacConville and McQuillan, like Osis and Haraldsson, also found that the calmness and consistency of the departing vision is nothing like erratic and random drug- or fever-induced delusions.

Instead of continuing to brush off the departing vision as a hallucination or by-product of the physiology of death, more modern-day researchers are beginning to scientifically explore the phenomenon. But because most medically trained individuals will only accept such information if it's presented in scientific studies, future investigations are needed.

MORE REBELS WITH A CAUSE

There have always been those professionals within the medical community who recognize the departing vision as a reality. Throughout the years I've received some incredible accounts from nurses and doctors. For example, several years ago I met a delightful nurse named Carla Helen Rockliff. As we talked I discovered she was not only a nurse educator, but also very aware of the departing vision. After Rockliff shared the way she handled a departing-vision event with a young dying patient of hers, I knew she was a true leader in her field. Today, her touching account (given in the following paragraphs) is used as an educational tool for teaching nurses about patient care and the departing vision.

During the winter of 1966, after a month of observing in the ICU at Boston Floating Hospital, I returned to Salem, Massachusetts, to set up a temporary ICU room at North Shore Babies' and Children's Hospital. It was around this time that a little boy, Jerry, was admitted by his pediatrician, Dr. C., who was our chief of staff. Dr. C. talked to me at length about this family and their love for all their children. His voice broke, and I could see tears as he spoke.

It had been arranged that I would care for his patient in the interim ICU room for the day shifts, Monday through Friday, and other nurses would be asked to fill in for the rest of the time. He could not tell how long it would be, but said that it was a terminal case. I was to use heart-monitoring equipment, oxygen, thermal blankets—whatever might be helpful for his care, and to keep him comfortable.

Jerry's pale blond hair and white skin reminded me immediately of Antoine de Saint-Exupery's *Little Prince*. He had been moved to North Shore to make it easier for his family to be close to him. It was a brain tumor that was taking the life of this beautiful 4-year-old.

Jerry's mom and dad took turns coming in early on the day shift and staying well into the evening. I had noticed that although Jerry was reaching the stage of coma, there were little lines of worry between his eyes and in his lips.

One Monday morning, I arrived to find that Jerry had not responded all weekend. There was an order for us not to resuscitate if he stopped breathing. The other nurses didn't feel adequate to take care of such a sick child when the end was so near. Checking his vital signs, I found that his pulse was thready and very low—only 42. I counted his respirations for a full minute—only eight.

Suddenly, for the first time in more than two weeks, Jerry sat straight up. He had been absolutely stiff, with no movement for so long, I couldn't believe it, and ran to his side.

His head turned to the right, his eyes moving, following something. "She's here!" his sweet little voice exclaimed.

I put my arms around his tiny shoulders and looked in the same direction, seeing nothing, but feeling tremendous warmth.

"Who is it, Jerry? Who do you see?" I asked.

"The pretty lady. Not my mommy."

He stretched out his right arm with delicate fingers trembling. I held his left hand in mine for support. "I love my mommy too," Jerry added.

"Your mommy and daddy love you too, Jerry. They'll be here in just a few minutes."

I wanted to reassure him. He was still looking to the right but smiling. The little lines of worry were completely gone. His blond head brushed my shoulder, and I lowered it to the pillow. The smile continued, but his breathing did not. This little prince was with his guardian angel.

Caring for each of my adult and pediatric patients certainly offered new experiences that I would use in my future work, but caring for Jerry will linger in my mind forever.[9]

Ms. Rockliff also had a near-death experience when she was very ill, and being an afterlife experiencer herself has helped her to better assist patients who have departing visions. Medical healthcare providers who personally encounter departing visions, after-death communications, or near-death experiences are often the best medical professionals in the field.

Similar to Ms. Rockliff, the nurse in the following example, whom I call Ms. A., also witnessed a powerful departing vision. This event changed the way she approached her patients who were getting ready to pass. Here is part of a letter she sent me.

When I try to tell others of the things I've seen, they may nod and murmur as if they understand, but at times I still feel very alone. Thank heavens for good friends who do listen and believe, and who have been comforted by what I have to say.

My mother passed after a short illness. We found out just a few days prior to her death that she had only a few days to live. She was given last rites and then came "alive" to have a "going away party." That was something else. We were able to take her home and, with hospice, care for her in her last days. What a wonderful experience this was. She talked with her mother and others who had passed many years before.

We asked my mother if she'd seen our dad and her response was, "Of course!" Witnessing her passing freed me from the fear of death, and your book gave me insight into those visits I've had from other deceased family members. Thank you for this, and keep up your writing, letting people know they're not crazy.

I'm a busy ER nurse and I've helped many to pass and hope to continue to do this as needed. I've had fellow nurses raise eyebrows when I talk with the deceased and when I say I'm doing so because I feel their presence and want them to know they're in good hands with God.

Thank you,

Ms. A.

The lessons she learned from her own mother's passing taught her how to be an even better healthcare provider. Not long ago, she shared this final thought with me, regarding two other books I've written on departing visions: "I am passing these on to fellow workers as this has been a year of loss for several of us and I'm hoping your books will give them some solace as well."

When it comes to understanding the departing vision and assisting patients, Ms. A. has gone against the professional grain. In caring for the dying she is very clear that death is just a transition, we are more than just the physical body, and our soul survives.

MEDICATION AND VISIONS

As more professional caretakers and studies confirm that the departing vision is real and not a result of the body dying or pain management medications, controversy about end-of-life care will increase. In the following study from India we again learn what nurses Rockliff and Ms. A. already know: Medical conditions and end-of-life medications are not responsible for the departing vision.

This is an interview-based study of 104 families and their observations of the last weeks and days of a dying family member. Forty families reported "unusual experiences and behaviors" from the dying person in their last period of life. Thirty of these dying persons displayed behavior consistent with deathbed visions—interacting or speaking with deceased relatives, mostly their dead parents. There were six cases of reported premonitions of death and five possible confusional states with one patient reported to have had both a deathbed vision and confusional experiences. Socio-demographic factors such as gender, age, occupation, or cause and place of death were not found to be significant. Hindu patients appeared to be more likely than Muslim patients to report these experiences. Use of opiates (or not) did not appear to influence reports. The findings are discussed with reference to past studies of deathbed visions as well as their implications for the future pastoral care of dying people and their families.[10]

Here we have one more interesting piece of research contradicting the belief that opiates, a family of medications traditionally used to manage severe pain, influence departing vision reports. Still, many medical professionals blame these visions on medications. I've unfortunately witnessed this myself on numerous occasions in hospital, hospice, and nursing home settings: A dying individual begins to experience the comfort and reassurance of the departing vision, and when family and friends ask, "What is this?" they are told it's "just the medication." In my experience, the physically dying who are not on pain medicine can have departing visions that are consistent with those individuals who are being given medications. These visions appear to be independent of the medicines administered at the end of life.

THE MILITARY STEPS IN

I am constantly reviewing the latest research for new information on the departing vision. Professionally speaking, I believe the more studies the merrier, especially for those of us who work with the dying and their families. While looking into the latest crop of studies, I was pleasantly surprised to discover that even the military was involved in departing-vision research.

Centuries ago these visions among military personnel were often the subject of books. Back then, unlike today, with Internet, texting, overnight mail, e-mail, and overseas telephoning, correspondences between members of the military and their family members could take a very long time. I remember my grandmother telling me how during World War II news of my uncle's tragic death in Germany didn't reach her for months.

Throughout the last decades I've read numerous accounts of wives, children, and parents receiving visitations from the spirit of their departing husband, father, son, brother, or friend, in the military, away at war. As with most visitations, these departing souls come to announce their passing and say goodbye or let dear ones know they are loved. Men overseas serving in the military have also encountered departing visions. These spiritual announcements were almost always related to a passing occurring at home. Read the following historical military departing vision to see what I mean.

In 1845 I was with my regiment in Maulmain, Burma. In those days there was no direct mail; sailing vessels brought us our letters, and months often went by without our receiving any.

The evening of March 24, 1845, I was dining with some other people at the home of a friend. Seated on the veranda after dinner, with other guests, I was talking of local matters, when suddenly I saw before me, distinctly, a coffin, and, stretched out in this coffin with every appearance of being dead, was one of my sisters, especially beloved, who was then at home. It goes without saying that I stopped speaking, and everyone looked at me questioningly. They asked me what was the matter. Laughingly I told what I had seen and my story was taken as a jest. In the course of the evening, in the company of an officer much older than I...I went back to where I lived. He (a captain in the military) returned to the subject, and asked me if I had received news that my sister was ill. I replied in the negative, adding that my latest letters from home were those I had received three months previously. He asked me to make a note of the vision because he had heard of similar experiences. I did this, making a note of it on a calendar opposite the date. On the seventh of the following May I received a letter telling me that my sister had died on the very day of that vision.[11]

The sister who passed in this account was in England while her brother was serving in the military in Burma. This spiritual message traveled more than 5,000 miles. Today, the power of historical military departing visions is being validated by modern-day research.

In working with dying members of the military, the director of palliative care services for the Veterans Administration with the Palo Alto Health Care Systems, Dr. James L. Hallenbeck, has calculated that approximately 25 percent of the dying encounter a departing vision.[12]

I'm so grateful for these studies, and for medical providers such as Dr. Hallenbeck who recognize the value of the departing vision. As opposed to being indifferent when patients or their family share accounts, these professionals have decided to take a closer look. And I'm not the only one, as the following letter from therapist Michael Kivinen to me makes clear.

> Carla,
>
> I've just listened to the first segment of your "2011 Coast-to-Coast AM" appearance, and found your perspective most refreshing. As a therapist working at an addiction treatment center I too encounter many clients who are struggling with trauma, grief, etc. When conducting assessments I've long made a practice of inquiring whether the client has ever had any psychic or paranormal experiences.
>
> When clients report them, they almost always preface their accounts with some variation on "I know this sounds crazy, but...." I am grateful to be

in a position to validate their experiences and help them integrate them. This includes clients who did not otherwise exhibit symptoms of schizophrenia, such as deterioration of functioning, but who began "hearing voices" of a deceased loved one. Biological psychiatry would be way too quick to medicate this experience as a psychosis, and conventional psychology would, at best, view it as an "introject" identification or (worse yet) "denial."

I've found instead that taking the experience seriously, treating it as normal, and facilitating communication between the client and what may very well be the voice of their departed loved one works quite well.

Please keep up your important work.

Michael K. Kivinen, MA, LLP, Therapist

Researchers and healthcare professionals such as Michael who continue to accept and explore afterlife experiences are slowly chipping away at the death phobia permeating our society. Addressing this taboo will not only aid the dying and their families, but will also begin to address another societal fear: the fear of aging.

The fear of aging has its iron-fisted grip on many of us today. I believe our obsession with excessive plastic surgery, so-called fountain of youth health supplements, and fear of ageism is tied directly to the boogieman we have turned the dying process into. Instead of looking at physical death as a natural transition and aging as a sign of a life well lived, we see each wrinkle as another nail in the coffin. Because of this, spirituality suffers.

Continued research into the departing vision will eventually relieve us of these time-consuming phobias. When this happens, our lives will no longer be ruled by fear. Instead, we will live each day to the fullest, filling every moment with what's really important.

CHAPTER 6

Dreamtime Premonitions

We sometimes congratulate ourselves at the moment of waking from a troubled dream; it may be so the moment after death.

—Nathaniel Hawthorne

As we have seen, departing visions occur every day, all around the world, and modern-day researchers are beginning to take such reports more seriously. As the Baby Boomer generation begins to age, retire, and then pass on, palliative care and hospice will become even more needed. These institutions, along with clergy and mental health organizations, must begin to accept that there is more to dying than just physical death. By recognizing that the departing vision is real and not the result of medications, medical conditions, or psychological pathology, the dying process can begin to take on new, spiritual meaning.

One area of the departing vision experience in need of more research involves the dreamtime encounter. For a beautiful description of what a dreamtime departing vision looks like, read the following account from 1899.

> One of my friends had a dream during the night, in which she saw one of her brothers, whom she tenderly loved, and whom she had not seen for a long time; he was dressed in white, he had a fresh complexion, and he seemed happy; the room in which she found him was also hung with white, and was filled with people; the brother and sister embraced each other affectionately.
>
> When her dream was ended, my friend awoke, and had a presentiment that her brother was dead. At that moment it struck midnight. The next day this lady learned by letter that her brother had died that night, exactly at midnight.[1]

WHAT DO OUR DREAMS TELL US?

This account is similar to a few of the departing visions I've personally experienced, in which these powerful "sleepytime" visitations coincide with the passing of a loved one. In many cases the person experiencing a dreamtime departing vision has no idea the dying loved one or friend is nearing physical death. Many of my peers in the field of mental health tell me such occurrences are just a coincidence. I continue to tell them we will need to "agree to disagree."

The "experts" have been arguing about the purpose of dreams for centuries. There are those scientists who believe dreams are random, senseless physiological experiences, which are nothing more than a by-product of the brain stem. Mental healthcare professionals, such as the father of psychiatry, Sigmund Freud, often see all dreams as having some deep psychological meaning. Some mental health caregivers will spend several therapy sessions with a client dissecting one particular dream.

Then there are the self-proclaimed dream interpreters. Modern-day dream mystics often assume the symbolism found in our sleepy time visions has just one or two interpretations. Each one of these so-called dream experts will put their own spin on what a particular symbol might mean. In the majority of cases, these individuals aren't medical or mental healthcare professionals, but instead advertise themselves as professional dream counselors, psychics, spiritual advisors, dream coaches, sleep technicians, and even regression therapists. The business of dream interpretation is big money, and a 45-minute session can cost as much as $100.

What might I get for my hard-earned cash? If I've had a dream about my teeth falling out, one interpreter might tell me I'm anxious about something. Another dream counselor could say my anxiety is about how I look. A third would tell me my dream is a warning about making costly mistakes. If I happen to be going through menopause, dreaming about my teeth falling out might mean I'm fearful of getting older. To be honest, the only time I've ever had a dream about my teeth was after a root canal!

I do believe our dreams keep us healthy. Dreamtime helps us process the stresses of the day. For most of my professional life, I've worked with trauma survivors, and I've noted that feelings related to unaddressed tragedy or loss will often appear in dreams. This is not unusual.

When I first started assisting clients suffering from trauma, I read a lot of books on dreams. In frustration, I ended up throwing most of them out. Too many of the authors thought they were better at interpreting my dreams than I was. Secondly, their explanations rarely fit for any of my clients. I finally realized these amateur interpretations were often based on the personal experiences, philosophies, and even religion of the dream counselors who wrote the books. With this new awareness, I came up with my own guidelines for understanding dreams.

LOOKING AT YOUR DREAMS

First, it's essential to know we are the best source for interpreting our own dreams. Symbolism found in my dreams will be different from yours. For example, I live on the Gulf Coast, so if I'm dreaming about hurricanes, it could be related to the large storm that dumped 10 feet of water into my house a few years ago. If *you* dream about hurricanes (and don't live in storm country), for you this might represent emotional turmoil. I've found it useful to write my nighttime visions out on paper. Then, for each line of the written-out dream, I go back and assign meaning as it relates to me.

Secondly, dreams help us work out our daily stress. Every once in a while I dream about flunking out of college. I've got years of post-college graduate work behind me and several degrees under my belt—obviously my dream isn't a literal premonition of things to come. For me personally, this sort of dream is a warning from my own subconscious that I've got too much stress in my life and I need to slow down. If my youngest son has dreams about flunking out of college, his experience is based in reality because he is in college! Dream symbolism will be different for each of us.

Also, as mentioned earlier, there are those dreams related to serious distress and upset. As a child I experienced a great deal of trauma and loss. For about a decade I had reoccurring nightmares related to my own tragic childhood history. Typically I would wake up from these nightmares scared and sweating profusely. Once awake it would take me a moment to realize I was no longer living in my past trauma. It was important for me to do the healing work necessary to relieve myself of these recurring nightmares.

Trauma can include emotional, physical, or sexual abuse, war, witnessing violence, or experiencing tragic loss or any other post-traumatic stress–inducing experiences. When we do the work to heal our traumatic encounters, our nightmares begin to dissipate. (For more information on this, read my book *Learning to Say No: Establishing Healthy Boundaries*.)

Children often experience recurring nightmares. These can be connected to trauma, but more often than not it's just stress. Such dreams are more likely about the trials of growing up and having new, challenging life experiences.

Finally, we have dreamtime encounters that are related to spiritual contact from the other side or premonitions of things to come. Skeptics tell us any dreams we have about the afterlife are related to grief, loss, and wishful thinking about a life after death. Some of our dreams about death are related to loss, and we can't ignore this. They are similar to stress or even trauma dreams. Then there are those dreamtime experiences that involve afterlife contact. Let's look at a dream visitation experience I had with my grandmother.

My grandmother Bertha was a tall, statuesque woman with shocking white hair piled high on her head. The daughter of immigrants from Russia, she had heard tales from her older sister and parents about relatives who had starved to death or were murdered by the Bolsheviks in the old country. In response to this, she worked hard at being an American and would decorate the house for every holiday celebrated in the United States. It wasn't uncommon for me to walk into her kitchen on Valentine's Day and find her baking fragrant Russian delicacies along with homemade heart-shaped sugar cookies!

When my mother died, I went to live with my grandparents. She taught me how to sew and put on lipstick, and every week we visited the local drug store for banana splits. She stepped right into my mother's shoes.

My grandmother passed when I was in my early 40s, so she had been part of my life for many years. Grief struck, and I didn't know how I'd continue without her. I'd cry uncontrollably while making Russian pies. During this time my poor family prayed for tacos, or a nice lasagna!

One night I had an incredible dream about my grandmother. In the dream I found myself in her very American kitchen. All of the colors were brilliant. Even the flowers growing just outside the window were incredible. The colors were so intense. Sitting at the kitchen table I was mourning the loss of my grandmother, when suddenly, in she walks.

In the dream, she was wearing a straight, shimmering purple number with long, graceful fitted sleeves. I can still hear the click of her purple high-heeled shoes as she walked up to me, pulled me out of my seat, shook me by my shoulders, and said, "Enough of this already."

My grandmother sternly reminded me that I had two young sons to take care of and that I didn't need to still be grieving for her. She told me she was just fine. After that she turned around and left me standing in the middle of her kitchen with my mouth wide open!

When I woke up I felt energized and knew my grieving time was over. I got back into my life and emotionally returned to my husband and boys. In my soul I knew my grandmother had come to me to set me straight!

Dreams involving afterlife contact leave us with feelings that are difficult to ignore. Following is a wonderful departing vision in the form of a dream from a confidential source who asked not to be named.

> I have a story to share that occurred with the passing of my grandmother. According to the doctors, she died around 3 a.m.
>
> That night I dreamed of her passing. I dreamt that I was driving home and passing by her house late at night when I had to stop to allow a funeral procession to pass in front of me. Interestingly my cousin said that she too woke up at 3 a.m. that night and stared at the clock.

In this account we see how two family members in different locations woke up at the moment of the grandmother's passing! When we've had an afterlife contact experience in a dream we know we've been touched by something special; it doesn't feel like a regular dream. Instead, we are left with a sense that life after death is real and our departed loved ones are still there for us.

Departing visions in dream form can also prepare us for a physical passing. Though this is the most common form of the departing vision, it is also the easiest for the skeptics to dismiss. The following example from a Jewish family really drives this notion home!

> In late December of 1978, my mother told me about a strange dream she recently had. It seems that in her dream, someone was knocking on our front door and trying to get in. According to my mother, she and I were trying to hold the door so

the person would not get in. She was, quite frankly, terrified because the person at the door had come for my father.

Well, as fate would have it, he suddenly passed away (at age 60) only a few days later. So, I guess that was sort of a "portent of fate."

I feel for the poor woman who had this dream. She was totally unprepared for the experience. Every once in a while a departing vision in dream form can be a frightening experience. None of us wants to suddenly lose someone we love. The husband passed away without warning, which suggests the family wasn't expecting his death to come anytime soon.

Having a dream of this sort would be very unnerving, especially if the experiencer was not familiar with this sort of encounter. In the following account, the dreamer is more prepared than the wife in the previous example, but her nighttime vision still leaves her feeling concerned.

I...never [lived] more than eight houses away from my first cousin and very best friend.... She was exactly six months older than me to the day. From the day were born, our mothers dressed us alike, did our hair alike, and signed us up for all the same after-school activities. We were more like twins than cousins. We attended [college] together, and lived in the same dorm as well. My cousin went on to med school and I went to work after graduation, and even though we each led our busy lives, we always remained close. We were maids of honor at each other's weddings, and the list goes on.

In her early 30s, my cousin was diagnosed with breast cancer. In the beginning, I was there for her every moment, but as her treatments progressed her mother started setting limits on my phone calls and visits.... Loving her as much as I did (and still do) I respected my aunt's wishes and started calling less and going to see her less.

My cousin's battle with breast cancer lasted a number of years. I was told that she had finally beat it, and was doing just fine and had in fact gone back to work and moved into a beautiful new condo. I was elated, hoping to soon resume our relationship, but I thought I'd take it slowly with her.

Two winters ago, I went on a trip with my family and I distinctly remember two days before coming home feeling very out of sorts. I was upset...I was tearful, and I finally put myself to bed only to have the most incredible dream.

I dreamt I was walking down a very long hallway and it was unbelievably bright white on all sides. My cousin was walking behind me and the whole way down the hall I kept looking over my shoulder at her saying, "Come on! I have to show you something! Come on!" In the dream I was so happy for my cousin, like something wonderful was going to happen to her.

I led her to a set of huge double doors. They were just as white and bright as the rest of the hall. As I stood in front of these doors, I threw them open for her. The room on the other side was filled with the most magnificent flowers you've ever seen. I didn't go in the room but I kept saying to my cousin, "Look! All of these flowers are for you! They're all for you!"

In the dream my cousin was in awe. She kept looking at the flowers and at me, saying, "For me? They're for me?" And I replied, "Yes sweetie, all for you."

When I woke the next morning I was so upset by this dream that I called my mother at 7 in the morning to tell her about it. That night, I went to bed and woke up at around 2 in the morning to one of my kids getting sick. I put him back to bed but I couldn't sleep. I was upset, extremely agitated and tearful, thinking about the dream I'd had the night before. My husband could not figure out was going on with me.

I specifically remember looking at the clock and noting that it was 2:20 a.m. The next morning, I got a phone call from my brother back home that my cousin had passed away the night before at 2:20 a.m.

Even though this experiencer was unaware her beloved best friend and cousin was so ill, her mood and dream told her something else.

When someone we love moves from this life to the next, before knowing they have passed on we may find ourselves feeling tearful, agitated, uncomfortable, or distressed. Sometimes these empathetic feelings can include physical symptoms. Here's an example from my own life.

When my mother was being taken from our home in an ambulance, I was at a rock concert. While cheering for my favorite band, I suddenly felt ill. I found an ambulance just outside the gates of the concert and crawled on in! After lying down, I slept through the concert. Once I woke up and returned home, I learned an ambulance had come to our home to take my mother away. She passed shortly after this.

I believe I was experiencing what was happening to my mother as she prepared to move on to the afterlife. Since then, I've become very teary and agitated when a loved one is about to pass, and, similar to the previous experiencer, I have almost always been validated by a phone call after the physical death has occurred.

Survivors aren't the only ones to dream about an upcoming passing; those who are about to leave this life can also be forewarned with a dream. The next account is a great example.

In 2011, a rock-'n-roll star, Mikey Welsh, former bassist of American alternative band Weezer, had a dreamtime premonition that told him to tie up loose ends. Welsh had played with the group from 2000 to 2001, when he had to end his career with Weezer after a drug overdose and attempted suicide. Welsh checked himself into a psychiatric hospital, and, after treatment, decided to retire from music to pursue a career in art. On September 26, 2011, Welsh dreamt he would die of a heart attack in his sleep in Chicago in a couple of weeks. He even posted this on Twitter:

"dreamt i died in chicago next weekend (heart attack in my sleep). need to write my will today"

"correction—the weekend after next"[2]

Welsh was found in his room at the Raffaello Hotel in Chicago, dead from a heart attack brought on by a drug overdose several weeks later.

Was this a planned suicide? There has been much debate about this because Welsh had a long history of drug abuse and mental illness. Having been in my own recovery from substance abuse for almost 30 years, I know what my future would have been if I hadn't gotten sober in 1984. In Welsh's case, what caught my eye was his predicted cause of physical death: a heart attack in his sleep.

Before leaving his wife and two sons in Vermont and traveling to Chicago to see his former band buddies perform at the Riot Fest the next day, he posted this on Facebook: "I'm excited to see the boys, hang out and have some fun."[3] There is no indication of suicidal thinking or behavior in this post. After landing in the Windy City he then remarked on Facebook that he was very happy, liked Chicago, and added the following: "I'm pretty much going to concentrate on my drawings while I'm here."[4]

This tells me he wasn't planning on dying in Chicago. No, the 40-year-old Welsh was looking forward to not only seeing his friends, but also spending time on his creative art. Sadly, two weeks after his premonition of death by heart attack, the disease of chemical dependency caught up with him and he passed as predicted.

I wonder if Welsh did listen to his dreamtime departing vision and took the action necessary to prepare for his death. Some experiencers do try to act on their premonitions. For example, Cincinnatian David Booth also experienced dreamtime departing visions. In 1979 he contacted the Federal Aviation Administration and told them he'd been having dreams about a devastating airline crash:

> He described the type of aircraft, its color, and the airline, but did not know where and when the accident would occur. The details of his dream, however, proved accurate when, a week later, an airliner lost an engine as it was taking off from Chicago's O'Hare airport and crashed, killing all on board. Two passengers who had booked seats on the flight had cancelled. They were actress Lindsay Wagner and her mother. Wagner had also had a premonition about the flight.[5]

Lindsay Wagner is an Emmy award–winning actress best known for her role in the popular television program *The Bionic Woman*. Today she gives workshops on meditation and holistic living. Her seminars are very popular, and if she hadn't cancelled her flight more than four decades ago, her fans would not be benefiting from the spiritual messages she is sharing today.

How can those who believe our dreams are purely biological or psychological explain Ms. Wagner and Mr. Booth's identical departing visions? The two didn't know one another or discuss their visions before the flight. Such fantastic premonitions can't be so easily dismissed!

TRUSTING YOURSELF

Dreams of this nature affect us spiritually for the rest of our lives. When we experience such dreamtime visitations we awake confident that there is more to our existence than just this life. Staying true to ourselves after a departing vision can be difficult. As society's values impinge upon our reality we may find ourselves questioning our afterlife contact. If you have a departing-vision dream, write it down and date it. By reliving every detail of the experience, you will again be reminded that what you encountered was truly spiritual in nature.

DISASTROUS DREAMTIME DEPARTING VISIONS

When the space shuttle *Challenger* exploded and then disintegrated over the Atlantic Ocean just off the coast of central Florida on January 28, 1986, my husband, Michael Brandon, a clinical psychologist, and I were very involved in providing grief and trauma support to the NASA community. Many of the peers, friends, and family of the *Challenger* crew suffered from post-traumatic stress disorder (or PTSD). Dreams associated with the trauma of this tragic disaster were very common among them, and extensive psychological work was needed.

Previous to the *Challenger* disaster, I'd heard my fair share of departing visions, and though I specialized in trauma, about this same time I began investigating departing visions more seriously. After the tragedy, I began hearing from experiencers who had had departing-vision premonitions about the disaster before it happened. Even an acquaintance of mine told me he'd had a vision about the shuttle's misfortune before the catastrophe occurred. Many of these accounts sounded like Chantel Lysette's experience, documented in her book, *Azrael Loves Chocolate, Michael's a Jock: An Insider's Guide to What Your Angels Are Really Like*. In that book Lysette shares with her readers a powerful dreamtime departing vision that took place in 1986 when she was just 12 years old:

> I was in bed catching a last few minutes of sleep before rising for school, and dreaming I was watching the news on television. A space shuttle had just been launched, but the anchorman became hysterical and began reporting that the shuttle had exploded. I was a bit shaken when I awoke, but I quickly dismissed the dream—not only did I not have plans to be on a space shuttle anytime soon, but I was hardly interested in the U.S. space program at the time.

> Later that day, an announcement came over the school's PA system that the space shuttle *Challenger* had exploded just seconds after launch. At the time, I didn't put two and two together. In fact, I remember thinking, *What exploded?* I'd had no prior knowledge that a shuttle was being launched. The only thing on my mind at the time was what mom might have been cooking for dinner and if my favorite rerun of *The Jeffersons* was coming on.

> Well, to my dismay, there was no rerun of *The Jeffersons* on when I got home. Instead, I found myself staring at continuous replays of the *Challenger* tragedy on television. A few hours passed before

I remembered the dream—and when I did, a chill moved through me. I tried telling my mother about the dream, but her reply did little to allay my fears.

"Sometimes it just happens," she said. "You'll see things before they come to pass. I get that all the time."[6]

In Lysette's vivid dream she experienced a powerful departing vision. Her mother comforted her and shared how she herself also had visions just like this.

Emotionally and even physically the sensations of this sort of departing vision tend to be intense, and there is a strong awareness that this isn't an everyday dream. Departing visions foretelling major disasters feel very real and then come true. Everyday stress dreams about living people don't feel the same.

Months before the 9/11 bombings occurred, Chris Robinson, an acquaintance of mine in England, had dreams about possible terrorist attacks in the United States. Then, in August of 2001, when Chris was in Tucson, Arizona, he began having horrific dreams about planes crashing into buildings in New York City. He was very upset and concerned. In his dreams, thousands of people were going to die.

Once back home in England the dreams continued, so Chris began recording his premonitions and even drew pictures of what he was seeing. Shaken by his dreams, he even contacted the authorities. Several days before the devastating al-Qaeda bombings Chris went so far as to send a letter to the London Embassy, warning that a terrorist attack in the United States was imminent.

Because Chris had been working with authorities as a psychic in London, copies of his drawings depicting planes crashing into tall building in New York City were documented. Journalist and author Gary S. Bekkum reported several premonitions regarding the 9/11 bombings. The following information about Chris Robinson's premonitions comes from two of his articles.

UK-based Christopher Robinson—a psychic with a history of providing warnings of terrorist events before they take place—confirmed to me he provided the U.S. Central Intelligence Agency Special Operations Intelligence Officer at the U.S. Embassy a warning that terrorists were about to use passenger planes as "cruise missiles"—something his previous handlers at MI5 (the British Security Service) could not accept.

According to Robinson, visions of the use of passenger planes as weapons of mass destruction began in 1999.

Robinson recently confirmed his intelligence contact in the UK:

"I reported the use of civil airliners as cruise missiles first in June 1999—6 June [1999] to be exact—to an officer with a UK department for intelligence gathering. His name is Mr. McElroy and he reported it to his boss—and both of them later came to a face-to-face meeting with me, and [they] confirmed that other intel people were very interested in what I had seen."[7]

January 2001: Psychic "dream detective" source Chris Robinson, concerned about dreams of an air attack against Western targets involving hijacked aircraft, has a falling out with his MI5 (U.K. Military Intelligence, Section 5) handler. Robinson is determined to prove the reality of his future visions, and decides to seek academic support in the United States. Although aware of new terror threats from al-Qaeda, Bekkum shelves a private future-directed investigation during a contentious divorce, unaware of Mr. Robinson's concerns.

August 2001: Chris Robinson's psychic vision is tested at the University of Arizona by Professor Gary E. Schwartz. During his stay in the United States, Robinson has increasingly intense visions of the 9/11 attack in New York City.

September 2001: Following his return to the United Kingdom, Robinson warns the U.S. CIA presence in London about his visions, hours before the actual attacks occur. During the attacks of September 11, Robinson is contacted by a U.S. Colonel (Col. John B. Alexander). Eventually Robinson will return to the United States, where he will meet with DIA and NSA operatives.[8]

About a decade ago, I too had an overwhelming dreamtime departing vision involving a terrible disaster. The experience created a multitude of emotions and questions for me about the nature of time and space—hearing such accounts from other experiencers was one thing;

being confronted with such a dramatic departing vision was another!

A month after 19 terrorists from the Islamist militant extremist group al-Qaeda hijacked passenger jets and intentionally crashed planes into the Twin Towers of the World Trade Center in New York City, the Pentagon in Arlington, Virginia, and a field near Shanksville, Pennsylvania, killing nearly 3,000 people, my husband and I were feeling overwhelmed, both personally and professionally.

Several of our clients had been at the World Trade Center before the attack. One family member was supposed to be lunching at the Trade Center at the time of the violent strike. Other family and friends watched the devastation from high-rise buildings in Manhattan. A cousin found himself walking from the Pentagon district to his home through miles of abandoned cars after the tragedy. Thankfully, all survived, but like millions of Americans and members of the global community, 9/11 will be forever imprinted upon our psyche.

On the morning of November 12, 2001, two months after the attacks, I was exhausted and decided to sleep in late. In the early morning hours I had what I thought was just a bizarre, stress-related dream. In the dream, a neighborhood was on fire. An airplane had made a crash landing, then exploded, and cinders were falling out of the sky. I found myself walking around the crash site taking in the frightening scene. Houses and buildings were on fire, and I could see the tail end of an airplane surround by flames and debris. Though I knew it was morning, the sky was filled with smoke and the skyline was very dark. Sirens blared and people were screaming. Others were running in all directions.

Suddenly, I saw people flying overhead like angels in the air, without wings. As they flew high in the sky many of them were looking down upon the tragedy with great sorrow. At first I couldn't understand who they were or what they were doing. Then, to my amazement, they spread their arms wide and began plummeting down into the scene of chaos below. As they flew through the horrific destruction, they began gently kissing the men, women, and children of the destroyed neighborhood on their foreheads. Such tenderness completely surprised me.

Though the surrounding devastation and destruction was nightmarish, this loving act of concern was a beautiful sight. As the dream continued, I remember thinking, "Oh, these poor souls are sad too. It must be heartbreaking for them to see how upset the survivors are."

After watching hundreds of these angel-like figures care for the survivors, I suddenly realized these were the souls of the individuals who had died in the plane crash. They were trying to comfort the neighborhood survivors. After leaving a kiss, they then looked upward, spread their arms even wider, and flew off, higher and higher until they had disappeared into the stars.

After this I woke up with tears in my eyes, feeling a deep sense of distress. Pulling my bedcovers up close around me, I reviewed the dream and thought, "This must be related to my own grief about 9/11," and then fell back to sleep for about an hour.

When I finally woke up, I got out of bed, threw on my bathrobe, and went downstairs for a cup of tea. The dream was still bothering me as the tea kettle began to whistle. After finishing my breakfast, I turned on the radio and heard a news report that left me feeling stunned.

At 9:17 EST on the morning of November 12, 2001, just two months after the 9/11 attacks, American Airlines Flight 587 crashed into the Belle Harbor neighborhood of Queens, a borough of New York City, shortly after takeoff from John F. Kennedy International Airport.

I quickly turned on the television, fearing this was another terrorist attack. What I saw on the screen frightened me. An airplane had indeed crashed into a neighborhood, and the scene was similar to my dream. The air was thick with smoke and people were in chaos. The houses in the neighborhood were lined up just as I'd seen them in my vision and there was destruction everywhere. Flames of fire shot up into the air and chaos permeated the landscape. Even the plane wreckage looked as it did in my dream. Later I would learn there had been 260 fatalities on board and five on the ground.

Terrorism was eventually officially ruled out as the cause of this particular disaster.

I'd awoken from my dream approximately one hour before the crash had occurred. Though I've had some incredibly powerful departing visions, this particular encounter, which involved a multitude of people I didn't even know, left me feeling overwhelmed for weeks. For me the experience reaffirmed that no matter how tragic a passing, life does not end with physical death, and love continues.

It took me some time to sort myself out after this experience. My beliefs were being challenged: I'd always considered myself to be a fairly run-of-the-mill, average person. Never in my life have I felt the need to advertise my services as a psychic. What I eventually recognized was that before any large-scale disaster, a strong spiritual energy begins to permeate the web connecting us to one another. I believe all of us are capable of receiving powerful premonitions of things to come.

To illustrate my point, following is a similar dreamtime departing vision. It too involves the 2001 airline crash in the neighborhood of Belle Harbor, Queens. This account comes to us from Sieg Pedde in Canada. He wrote about his vision in a letter to his son.

On November 12, 2001, I awoke at 7 a.m. or so with the memory of a very troubling dream. I reflected on it a bit before I got ready to go to the office, wondering what it meant, and what, if anything, I should do about it.

I dreamt that you and I were walking down a street. There were two-story buildings, mostly residential, on both sides of the street. There were lots of trees, just what one might expect in an older neighborhood in a large city. I don't know which direction we were facing, but when I glanced off to our right, past the houses and other buildings, I could see water. On the other side of the body of water, I could see a city skyline. To our left, past the buildings on the other side of the street, I could see water too. It was evident that we were on a peninsula of some kind, near an airport and a large city.

As we walked along the street, I sensed something was amiss. I looked up. Coming towards us, at an altitude consistent with just having taken off from an airport, I saw a large, commercial airliner. As I watched, the nose of the aircraft skewed to its left and the aircraft continued forward, towards us, in that unnatural position. I don't remember now if there was an explosion, or any visible fire that preceded what happened next, but the aircraft suddenly fell from the sky and landed on the ground, plowing through homes and other structures that were in its path. The buildings splintered as the aircraft slid through them. The plane started to break up and the conflagration that resulted soon covered what appeared to be an area approximately the size of a city block. Frightened, I grabbed your hand and we ran away from the mayhem. Then I woke.

I got to work at about 8:20 that morning. I debated whether to tell anyone about my dream. I often talk about my dreams because they are incredibly realistic, and, frankly, often entertaining. I think of my dreams as interesting, not as portents of things to come. On November 12, 2001, I decided against telling anyone of my dream. The terrorist hijackings of September 11, 2001 were still fresh in everyone's minds. I thought that my subconscious mind might still be dealing with the horror of the hijacked aircraft crashing into the Pentagon and the twin towers of the World Trade Center.

As I do every morning, I connected to the Internet to read my e-mail and to browse through the daily news via links on the Drudge Report and World Net Daily.

By approximately 10:00 a.m., the Internet was awash with reports of the crash of American Airlines flight 587. It had taken off from John F. Kennedy International Airport in New York at 9:13 a.m., and at 9:17 a.m. it crashed into an older neighborhood in the New York borough of Queens.

Much of what happened to Flight 587 eerily reflects the events in my dream. I won't go into a lot of detail here about the similarities; the crash information is a matter of public record and is available on the Internet.

For several days after the crash, I felt guilty, as though I should have reported the dream to someone. Perhaps some lives could have been saved. But reported to whom? Who would have listened? How could anyone know which plane, at which airport, in which country to focus on? Why would anyone believe that a dream, in advance of a later occurrence, would have any connection to the real event?

And how do I know that the dream was an omen, a premonition?

I don't. I have mentally filed the tragic events of that day, and the dream that preceded them, as yet more strange coincidences.

Neither Sieg nor I knew any of the victims in Queens, New York. And up until about a year ago we didn't know one another! In spite of this we had almost identical dreams about this disaster before it happened.

❁ ❁ ❁

There is so much we don't know about life after death, but in keeping an open mind we become more willing to explore and learn. When we heal our own death phobia we can then be of service to others. Both Sieg and I have openly shared our accounts to help those of you who may be confused about your own experiences.

As we have seen, not all of our dreams are related to physiology or our emotional state. Our dreamtime departing visions can be about physical death on a large scale, our own upcoming passing, or the transition of someone we love or care about. In the following departing vision account, sent to me in a letter from a woman named Victoria in Mississippi, all looks well, but a dream tells a different story.

I Googled the term "deathbed vision," and your name came up so many times that I felt compelled to write to you. On January 20, 2010, my mother was diagnosed with ovarian cancer. We were told that with surgery and chemo, her prognosis would be good. She had the surgery and was fine for several days. She was alert, talking, breathing fine, and appeared to be on the road to recovery. I stayed with her every night after her surgery, except for the days that she was in the ICU following surgery. About a week after surgery, I was asleep on the cot beside her, and I had the most vivid dream. She was in the same hospital room, except it was extremely bright and sunny, and the windows and door were made of glass. In my dream, my mom hugged me, told me she loved me, and said that she was going to die and she wanted to tell me goodbye. In my dream, she looked healthy and happy. I cried and hugged her and told her goodbye. The dream was so vivid that when I awoke, I was still crying and saying "bye mama." I even woke her up, and she said to me, "Why are you saying 'bye'?" I replied, "Nevermind, I was dreaming..." Two days later, the doctor told me that her vital signs and x-rays indicated that she would not make it out of the hospital and placed her in hospice care. Seven days later, at the age of 59, she died with me holding her hand.

At the time, I thought that this was something I had simply dreamed up or imagined, but the more I read, the more I discover that my mother actually came to me in my dream to comfort me and prepare me for her passing. She also had visions a few days before she died. One day, she said that there were people in her room and that they were all dead. She appeared to be frightened at first, but then calmed down....

I just wanted to share my story with you.... I am so comforted to know that our connection was so strong that she spoke to me in my dreams before she even passed away.

Some dream interpreters believe dreaming about a death means job loss or the end of a romantic relationship. This might be the case for some people, but it doesn't fit for Victoria's situation. I believe the spiritual essence of this mother wanted to prepare her daughter for her upcoming physical passing. This is love, and love transcends the material world. Both mother and daughter were comforted and neither experience can be explained away with physiology, psychology, or simple dream analysis. Something much more spiritual was happening.

The following dream is another perfect example of what I'm saying. This particular account comes from an elderly man who corresponded with me a number of years ago. Throughout his life he had departing visions and premonitions and often shared these with family and friends.

I thought you might be interested in a happening that occurred a few months ago. I had several heart surgeries and a major heart attack. I was neither depressed nor afraid of dying. While I was in intensive care, I had a visitation that might be of interest to you.

To give you a little background, my best friend for more than 60 years, died last year after a prolonged illness. His story is a tragic one. He was predeceased by both of his children and his wife. His life was frequently compared to that of Job in the Bible.

I was asleep in intensive care and in my dreams I saw a river. One side was very dark and the other was extremely bright. The bright side was beautiful, with green grass, rolling hills, etc. I was on the dark side. Suddenly my friend and his wife appeared with one of their children on the bright side of the river. He and his wife were holding hands and all of them were smiling and laughing. My mother and father (now both deceased) also appeared, smiling, laughing, and waving. A little boy was with them. I have previously seen this child with them. I believe the boy to be my grandson who died at birth.

My maternal grandmother and one of my maternal aunts were also there, smiling, laughing, and waving. My friend (from the other side of the river) spoke to me and said, "When the time comes, my wife and I will take you across the river." I awoke, not frightened, but kind of peaceful. As I said I was not afraid of dying before the visitation and certainly not afterwards.

When we experience encounters of this nature, any fear we may harbor about permanent separation from those we cherish evaporates. One day we will reunite with those who have gone before us. Dream time visitations assure us the journey continues and let us know our loved ones are just a breath away.

CHAPTER 7

Visitations at the Moment of Death

Between deaths and apparitions of the dying person a connection exists which is not due to chance.
—H. Addington Bruce

As we saw in the last chapter, afterlife contact can come in the form of dreams. These wonderful communications provide a great deal of hope, letting grieving family and friends know, "I'm not dead! I'm still here! All is well and I love you!" But afterlife encounters also show us that departing visions are occurring when the experiencer is fully awake. This powerful type of visitation is often bestowed upon family members and friends at the time of a loved one's physical death—when no one knew the person has died! Read the following to see what I mean.

I'm always looking for explanations about what I experienced because I know for sure that I experienced something. The first time this happened to me was with my mother's father. He had a stroke and was lying in bed in the living room of the house. We were all taking turns sitting with him and on the night he died I was with him early in the evening and talking to him. Well, I went home and was sitting at my kitchen table when all of a sudden I felt this strange sensation (hard to explain but it was like I felt my grandfather's presence); I looked up at the clock, saw the time, and then saw my grandfather's face kind of pass through me and rise toward the heavens.

I told my husband what had just happened and he said, "Then the phone should be ringing," and he no sooner got the words out of his mouth than the phone rang with the news that my grandfather died at the exact moment that I saw on the clock when I looked at it. I was wide awake. I hold this in my heart always and wonder, *Why me?* Out of everyone in the family why did I experience this? I thought of a lot of scientific explanations. One was that he was thinking of me as he died and I was thinking of him. But I know it was more than that really.

Such a precious spiritual greeting from a beloved grandfather will stay with her for the rest of her life.

Other departing visions from the past parallel this encounter. For example, in 1892, Reverend Matthew Frost of Bowers Gifford, Essex, provided an incredible account to a Professor Sidgwick. Being the first president of the Society for Psychical Research, naturally Sidgwick was very interested in what the reverend had to say. Following is the departing vision Reverend Frost shared with Professor Sidgwick.

The first Thursday in April, 1881, while sitting at tea with my back to the window and talking with my wife in the usual way, I plainly heard a rap at the window, and looking round at the window I said to my wife, 'Why, there's my grandmother,' and went to the door, but could not see anyone; still feeling sure it was my grandmother, and knowing, though she was 83 years of age, that she was very active and fond of a joke, I went round the house, but could not see anyone. My wife did not hear it. On the following Saturday, I had news my grandmother died in Yorkshire about half an hour before the time I heard the rapping. The last time I saw her alive I promised, if well, I would attend her funeral; that was some two years before. I was in good health and had no trouble, age 26 years. I did not know that my grandmother was ill.

Mrs. Frost writes: "I beg to certify that I perfectly remember all the circumstances my husband has named, but I heard and saw nothing myself."

Professor Sidgwick learned from Mr. Frost that the last occasion on which he had seen his grandmother, three years before the apparition, she promised if possible to appear to him at her death. He had no cause for anxiety on her account; news of the death came to him by letter, and both Mr. and Mrs. Frost were then struck by the coincidence. It was full daylight when Mr. Frost saw the figure and thought that his grandmother had unexpectedly arrived in the flesh and meant to surprise him. Had there been a real person Mrs. Frost would both have seen and heard; nor could a living person have got away in the time, as Mrs. Sidgwick found the house stood in a garden a good way back from the road, and Mr. Frost immediately went out to see if his grandmother was really there.[1]

The next historical account comes from a physician named Dr. Rowland Bowstead, of Caistor, England. Notice how similar it is to the previous two experiences: The moment a young man suddenly leaves this life for the next, his spiritual self is seen at another location by Dr. Rowland. In this particular case, 100 miles separated the physician from his beloved brother-in-law.

In September, 1847, I was playing at a cricket match, and took the place of long-field. A ball was driven in my direction which I ought to have caught but missed it, and it rolled towards a low hedge; I and another lad ran after it. When I got near the hedge I saw the apparition of my brother-in-law, who was much endeared to me, over the hedge, dressed in a shooting suit with a gun on his arm; he smiled and waved his hand at me. I called the attention of the other boy to it; but he did not see it, although he looked in the same direction. When I looked again the figure had vanished. I, feeling very sad at the time, went up to my uncle and told him of what I had seen; he took out his watch and noted the time, just ten minutes to 1 o'clock. Two days after I received a letter from my father informing me of the death of my brother-in-law, which took place at 10 minutes to 1. His death was singular, for on that morning he said he was much better and thought he should be able to shoot again.

Taking up his gun, he turned round to my father, asking him if he had sent for me, as he particularly wished to see me. My father replied the distance was too far and expense too great to send for me, it being over 100 miles. At this he put himself into a passion, and said he would see me in spite of them all, for he did not care for expense or distance. Suddenly a blood-vessel on his lungs burst, and he died at once. He was at the time dressed in a shooting suit and had his gun on his arm. I knew he was ill, but a letter from my father previous to the time I saw him told me he was improving and that he might get through the winter; but his disease was consumption, and he had bleeding from the lungs three months before his death.[2]

How on earth could the skeptics explain away these last three departing visions? Within our death-phobic society, finding traditional scientific explanations for these amazing visual afterlife encounters would be almost impossible, but I bet there are those who wouldn't think twice about trying. How do we make sense of this for ourselves?

TIMES AND PLACES

A nurse who has just read a magazine article of mine on departing visions sent me the following story in 2007. Again we have the physical body of a dying loved one in one location while his spiritual essence is in another.

I was working as a Certified Nurse's Assistant at a nursing home.... I was scheduled to leave work at 7, and as I was leaving I passed the room of a patient we knew was dying.

Alfred was a lovely man. He had lived his life well and deserved so much more than the way he was living now. It was a good facility, clean, sunny, and it even smelled like citrus and lavender. Though he was alone so much of the day, I knew trapped in his body was a man of thought and conviction. He was actually a bit intimidating to care for because of his beauty of spirit.

As I was leaving work, I saw a man at his bedside weeping. I almost left, but I felt his grief should not have to be borne alone. I walked in and told him, "We must help Alfred be more comfortable." So, I gathered the bath things and began washing Alfred's hand, then gave the man a wash cloth. We began to bathe Alfred with love and warm water.

He eventually opened up with, "I am his son." I asked him if he would like to pray, and that prayer will remain with me forever. "God, just please [pass] softly," he said. We began washing Alfred's face, his neck, his arms, and whispering over him for comfort and peace.

I asked the son to tell me about his dad, and he did. He told me how his father would walk him around their lake and how the ducks would call and scatter. He shared how Alfred was once so strong he could swing him around, and how he loved his wife. He told me his father was one of his heroes.

We were in Alfred's room for such a short time, only an hour or so. Then the next shift came on and interrupted our death ritual. By the time I left we were both in tears of joy over the life this man had led. As I was leaving, I heard Alfred's son whispering words of love and eternity....

I went home and cried in the shower, and then went to bed. In the middle of the night I awoke to find Alfred standing at the foot of my bed. He was so young and handsome.... I can't truly express the robust health of Alfred as he stood at the end of the bed. At the end of his life he was completely incapacitated. While in the nursing home Alfred had been wheelchair-bound, incontinent, had to be fed, and lacked speech. The Alfred I saw at the very end of my bed was physically larger than an actual person. It was almost as if he was trying to contain himself in his physical, earthly image for my benefit. Alfred looked so healthy and fit, and he had a pearl-like glow around him (not ghostly white or wispy but iridescent), and his eyes were so startlingly bright and there was only joy in them. It was like looking at eternity.

I was not frightened at all, and was hitting my husband saying, "Wake up! Wake up!" but he was sleeping so deeply, he missed it all.

Finally Alfred said, "Thank you for being with my son." Alfred then looked up to his left and said, "I have to go now, my Julia is waiting." I tried to stall him, but he said, "Oh Julia!" He glowed as he looked toward the left, toward Julia, and then became just light that transformed into glitter, floated upward, and was suddenly gone. I was sitting up, hitting my husband, and when he finally woke up he said, "What?" I asked him, "Did you see him?" He then asked what happened.

I got up and called the nursing home to ask about Alfred. A nurse told me he was fine, that she had just been in his room. Then I told her, "Check again! Alfred just died!" She did and came back to the phone and said, "I gotta go. He just died! He was pronounced dead while I was on the phone with you."

After Alfred died, his son came to see me and left me with a picture of him. The photo was wonderful but it didn't come close to the majestic, spiritual image of unconditional love and eternity I saw standing at the foot of my bed, glowing white with blue iridescent eyes. When he left, when he was going like glitter, the peace joy and relief of seeing his wife Julia, I can't even relate. This image will be forever etched into my mind.

I was awake, and this wasn't a dream. Until that night, because he wasn't my patient, I did not know his wife's name was Julia. [The son later let her know Julia was his mother.]

The topic of death is so very taboo in our culture. It is one of the few things we cannot control. We hide it away in hospitals, keep the children from seeing it, and do things like hush people. Instead we need to dance, weep, wail, and finally find comfort and peace.

Remembering this experience with Alfred, his wife, and son still makes me smile, and when I do remember, I always whisper a thank-you to this man for sharing with me a brief glimpse of the journey to the afterlife.

When I received this account, all I could say was, "Wow!" Here we have a departing vision report from a medical professional who didn't even know the dying patient. He just happened to be at a facility where she was employed. Yet his consciousness or soul traveled to her home to say thank you, because he was grateful for the care she provided to not only him, but also his son. Manners are a must, and he can't cross over completely until he expresses his gratitude.

Personal characteristics acquired in this life, like good manners, don't just fritter away with physical death. Along with this, bonds created with those we love will not dissolve. It has been my experience that this is especially true with children. Youngsters are often the first to be visited by a departing parent, grandparents, brother, or sister. Then they will talk of seeing what we as adults can't perceive. Sadly, our tendency is to dismiss this and go about our business. If a child is persistent we then tell ourselves it's just makebelieve and imagination. We think, "Just play along." In the following historical account we see how a mother tries to placate her young daughter after the child begins having visions of her dear brother.

On May 31, 1895, my eldest son, a volunteer with the first Hussars [a type of military cavalry], at Valence, was talking part in field maneuvers. Being at the head of the advance-guard, he was walking his horse...[and] a bullet struck my unhappy son full in the chest. Death came with almost lightning swiftness....

Now, that same day, May 31, 1895, about half-past nine in the morning, while my wife was at home, busy with household duties, our little daughter, then aged 2 and a half, went up to her mother and said in her childish speech, "Mamma, look at Godfather [my eldest son was his sister's godfather]; look; Mamma, look at Godfather. I'm having fun with him."

"Yes, darling, have your fun," her mother answered, attaching no importance to the child's words.

But the little girl, in the face of her mother's indifference, redoubled her insistence, and added, "But, Mamma, come and see Godfather. Look at him, he's there. Oh, how nicely he's dressed!"

Shortly before noon we received a telegram telling us of the terrible accident that had happened to our beloved son, and I found out later that this incident had occurred toward eight o'clock.[3]

Like so many parents in this situation, this mother gave little attention to what her daughter was saying. Only after verification of her son's untimely death did she realize the little girl truly was visited by her brother.

CHAPTER 8

Love Knows No Boundaries

There are no random acts. We are all connected. You can no more separate one life from another than you can separate a breeze from the wind.

—Mitch Albom

In researching departing visions, I had often wondered how it was possible for several people to have identical departing visions at the same time—such as when I was awakened early in the morning, along with my aunt, cousin, and two of my mother's friends, with a knowing that my mother had passed. For years I was

baffled as to how all five of us living in different locations could have had the exact same experience. One day
I had a vision of the web of life that clarified this for me.

Years ago I was driving home from the office and was
feeling bone-tired. I'd had an especially difficult day and
was wondering why it was my job to unravel the damage
we inflict upon one another. A young girl had just told
me her father had violently abused her, and earlier that
morning I'd spent time with a teen who had almost lost
her life to a serial rapist. As I cursed out the universe
over the inhumanity I'm so often confronted with, an
unexpected sense of calm came over me. Suddenly I had
a profound awareness that some sort of spiritual light was
weaving its way through all of us. In this vision I could
see how we were connected spiritually to one another,
to the universe, and to all of the solar systems in space.
For a brief moment, there was no sense of time or place.
Ideas of past, present, and future had no meaning.

This new spiritual awareness explained for me why so
many of us can have the same spiritual experience when
a loved one departs this world for the afterlife. We are
all spiritually connected!

THE BONDS OF LOVE

A number of years ago I had a delightfully com-
plicated friend. What a character this man was: rough
around the edges and anything but politically correct.
At times I actually cringed when he opened his mouth.
His wife put up with his antics for decades. She always
turned a blind eye when he acted up. Saying they had
a strange relationship is putting it mildly. This elderly

gentleman was not a "gentleman" in the conventional sense. But there were three things that few people knew about my friend: (1) He was incredibly well read and always had a stack of books on a variety of topics at his bed stand; (2) though friends would complain to me about the things he would say, he was always at the front of the line when someone needed help; and (3) he was deeply in love with his wife.

Once their children were grown and off raising their own families, my friend was looking forward to being the center of his wife's universe. Sadly, she became ill, and after several years, passed away. Left behind to fend for himself, this inwardly grieving husband put up a good front. Behind the bad jokes and attempts at shocking young women with his off-color attempts at flirting, I knew his grief was overtaking him. One night I had a dream about his wife. In this after-death communication she said to me, "Tell him he needs to pull himself together." From the other side she let me know she was worried about him. Several days later I saw him and decided to take a risk. I told him about this afterlife communication and tears welled up in his eyes. My share comforted him.

My friend didn't live much longer after that. Late one evening he passed from this life to the next with a smile on his face. Today I know he is with his beloved and I'm sure she's giving him grief every time he tells a bad joke!

Few marriages or partnerships survive today. Almost half of all couples walking down the aisle end up divorcing. Those who are willing to stick it out for better or worse, during times of joy and hurt, new beginnings and losses, develop bonds that tie them together for eternity.

One day I came across an amazing newspaper article that perfectly illustrates this. It talked about the bonds of love that continue after physical death. In Hanover, Pennsylvania, a man and wife who had been married for 61 years passed within hours of one another. They had raised six children together, had 10 grandchildren, and many great-grandchildren. He had been a truck driver, and after the kids were grown and gone she joined him in the front seat of his cab. Together they traveled the United States together. At 81 years of age, this devoted husband and family man discovered he was suffering from lung cancer. The family was naturally devastated, but tried to carry on. After a fall, the retired truck driver had to be hospitalized. The adult children feared they would need to move their father to a nursing home. This was something he had been adamantly against.

His beloved wife was naturally upset and didn't like being in the house without him. Soon she ended up in another hospital across town. A heart condition that had never been repaired eventually ended her life. The family hadn't planned on her going first. After her passing the grieving adult children knew they now needed to make the trip to the hospital across town and deliver the sad news to their father. After entering his room it was obvious that his time on this earth was also short. Twelve hours after their mother had passed on, their father was beginning to make his trip to the world to come. As they tried to feed him ice, his eyes were intently focused on the ceiling. He then said something that took his children totally by surprise:

"Pull me up," he whispered.

...he just said it again, over and over.

"Pull me up."

"Please, please pull me up...."

And then these words: "Hold me tighter now."

A minute later he was gone.

Off to be with the woman he fell in love with 60-plus years ago.... Two people, unable to be apart....[1]

I became misty-eyed when I first read this story and quickly passed it on to my husband.

When we or our loved ones leave this dimension and travel to the afterlife, those who have gone before us will be there to embrace us. We are never alone.

TECHNOLOGY'S ROLE

On October 5, 2011, Steve Jobs, the cofounder of Apple, died of pancreatic cancer. The world mourned the passing of this fascinating personality. Jobs's innovative creativity gave us the personalized computer, the iPod, iPhone, iPad, and so much more. His "outside the box" thinking also visually introduced us to what alternative dimensions might look like. With the development of cyberspace, he gave us a sneak peek at the multi-universe concept. (Today, with online games, neither of my sons have any difficulty understanding what an alternate dimension is.)

Several days after Jobs's passing, his sister Mona Simpson gave a heartfelt eulogy at her beloved brother's small, private funeral. Published in the *New York Times* on October 30, 2011, under the title, "A Sister's Eulogy for Steve Jobs," the piece ends with the following words: "Steve's final words, hours earlier, were monosyllables, repeated three times. Before embarking, he'd looked at his sister Patty, then for a long time at his children, then at his life's partner, Laurene, and then over their shoulders past them. Steve's final words were: "OH WOW. OH WOW. OH WOW.""[2]

As this technology icon was physically dying in his California home, what did he see over the shoulders of his family? Is it possible he was greeted by deceased loved ones? Was there a grand reunion? Did he finally see what the next dimension really looks like? Were his final words consoling to his grieving family? Did this leave them with a sense of hope? Do they understand that love continues? I sure do hope so.

A Songwriter's Vision

Popular American songwriter Johnny Cash often talked about the departing vision. I met Cash years ago while speaking at a conference in Arkansas.

Cash's 14-year-old brother, Jack, died a tragic physical death in 1944. Johnny, his mother, and Jack reported incredible premonitions.

One Saturday morning Johnny asked his brother to go fishing with him. Sadly, Jack went to work instead, and Johnny was left to go fishing by himself. Their mother knew something was wrong with Jack. She could tell he didn't want to go to work and said something to him about this. Jack told her and Johnny that the family needed the three dollars he would earn that day. She then again asked him to please not go. That day, while making fence posts at the high school, Jack had a tragic accident. Did Jack's mother have a premonition of things to come? I often wondered if the events of this day shaped not only Johnny Cash's musical career but also his spiritual philosophy. Here is his account.

At the fishing hole I spent a long time just sitting there, not even putting my line in the water. Eventually I cast, but I just played, slapping my line in the water, not even trying for a fish.

It was strange. It was as if I knew something was wrong, but I had no idea what. I wasn't even thinking about Jack; all I knew was that something wasn't right.... I got up, picked up my fishing pole, and started back home.

I saw my father.... I knew something was very wrong.... I just threw the pole in the ditch and got in the car.

"What's the matter, Daddy?" I asked.

"Jack's been hurt really bad," he said.

...the saw table had cut Jack from his ribs down through his belly, all the way to his groin....

On Friday Jack took a turn for the worse.

I woke up early on Saturday morning to the sound of Daddy crying and praying. I'd never seen him pray before, either. He saw me awake and said, "Come on into his room. Let's say goodbye to him."

...suddenly [Jack] grew calm and lucid. He looked around and said, "I'm glad you're all here."

He closed his eyes, "It's a beautiful river," he said. "It's going two ways.... No, I'm not going that way.... Yes, that's the way I'm going.... Aaaaw, Moma, can't you see it?"

"No, son, I can't see it," she said.

"Well, can't you hear the angels?" Tears came from his eyes. "I wish you could," he said. "They're so beautiful.... It's so wonderful, and what a beautiful place that I'm going."

...and he was gone.[3]

When a mother, father, brother, sister, grandparent, friend, lover, wife, husband, or child departs this life, many of us wonder, "Can we still have a loving connection with our dear ones, or do relationships end with death?" I don't believe physical death ends these loving relationships. History, religion, and modern-day stories of afterlife contact assures us that loving relationships continue. This is a universal experience. See the next account, sent to me by a confidential source.

Your information about departing visions left me feeling more comfortable with an experience I witnessed. My father died a couple of months ago, and we as a family really have been missing him. Just before he died, I remember feeling kind of strange. He died suddenly so I wasn't with him when he passed. I do know I just felt strange at the time of his death. I found out when he died later. Also, a couple of weeks before he died he started dreaming about his mother who had died a long time ago. He just kept dreaming about her.

This person's experience shows us how both the physically dying individual and the surviving family and friends can be touched by departing visions simultaneously. The daughter said she felt "strange" at the time of her father's passing even though she was unaware he was moving on.

A relative of mine passed just last month. At the time of his physical death I was unaware he was about to leave this life. During this same time I was very weepy but couldn't put my finger on why. Several weeks later I learned from a cousin that at the ripe age of 99 he had left his tired body for the afterlife. When I looked at the timeline, I clearly saw how my tearful state corresponded exactly with the day of his physical death. Let's look at another account tha demonstrates how survivors can be visited with premonitions of an upcoming passing.

Let me tell you about my experiences.... I am a Jewish male, age 72, who has had these "visitations" for many years. It is not uncommon for relatives and friends who are deceased to "visit" with me. Sometimes they deliver messages and sometimes they are just there. Also, many times I am awakened during the night, sit up in bed, and see these "forms" moving around the room.

Before experiencing my own departing visions, I would have scoffed at this account. Today such shares astonish me. This Jewish man's encounter once again shows us that communication between our physical world and the afterlife does continue and that the death of the body doesn't sever loving relationships. Our departed relatives don't abandon us. Love crosses all boundaries. They are right there with us, especially when we need them.

When I'm at the funeral of a family member or friend I often receive quick, sharp mental impressions of the physically departed being right there, looking to see who has come to the event! At times the comments I hear from these souls have made me chuckle. Once, a dear friend of mine in spirit form commented on one of the mourners attending his funeral. Suddenly I heard, "What is he doing here? He didn't like me when I was alive!" Shocked and surprised, I started to laugh out loud during a very solemn prayer!

Here is an afterlife contact experience similar to what I just shared with you.

> We were all pretty young when my grandfather died. There were about eight of us cousins who attended my grandfather's funeral and all of us were still in elementary school. He had lived a very long life so his death wasn't unexpected. Regardless, sitting there with my cousins I remember we shared a tissue box. He was well loved and we were going to miss him.

My grandfather was a World War II vet and I think he must have seen some pretty terrible sites in Europe, because he never did want to talk about those years. My grandmother had died ages ago and I don't think he ever recovered from this. But, in spite of his sadness he always loved seeing me and my cousins.

Our grandfather couldn't cook, but insisted on feeding us when we showed up for a visit. He liked to tease us with his food preferences. The sardines on crackers with peanut butter looked just awful, but he'd lap it up, and then chase it back with black coffee. He told me he ate a lot of peanut butter in the military and just happened to like sardines too. After torturing us with this concoction, he'd eventually bring out the cookies.

When he died he seemed too big for his casket and he really didn't look like himself. I had this feeling he was looking down on his body shaking his head and saying, "Too much make-up!"

Just as the service was about to begin, this good-looking couple walked up the aisle, to the casket, smiled, turned around, and then walked out the church. None of us knew who they were.

After the funeral we went to my aunt's for a bite to eat and decided to look through old photo albums. All of us kids were sitting on the floor and taking turns flipping through the old musty pages when one of my cousins found an old photograph and said, "Hey! Look what I found! Doesn't this picture look like that strange couple who showed up at the church?" All of us crowded around this one cousin and then someone said, "Look at the bottom of the picture. Those are the names of our great-grandparents! You don't think that was really them do you?" For a several seconds no one spoke. Finally someone said, "Let's look at another book," and the topic was never brought up again.

Did the children see their great-grandparents approach the grandfather's casket? The great-grandparents appeared to them as they did in the old photograph, when they were younger. Had they come to escort their son to the afterlife?

When we go through hard times, the physically departed can return to us in spirit form. Consciousness continues and it's this aspect of the soul that reaches out to comfort us during our time of need. With the passing of a dear one the bonds of love between the departed and the grieving aren't broken.

The following account brings this point home. A mother has left this dimension for the next, and her daughter has been extremely distraught. At the funeral her grief is softened when she feels her mother's loving touch. Afterward, she has difficulty putting the experience into words. This share comes from my cousin Betty.

Speaking of my mom, it was difficult to talk about my experience last night. Never knew there was a name for it. I have only told a few people. People who are close and knew were "safe" to talk to.

It happened just after I had asked myself, "Where am I going to get the strength to get through this funeral?" I then felt something touch my shoulders and suddenly a great sense of wellbeing filling up inside me. I stopped trembling and stopped being on the verge of tears. All felt calm and clear. For the rest of the funeral and burial experience I was back to being able to keep the crying and internal pain under control.

Some people would say it was the presence of God. The Catholics may draw strength from a particular saint. But for me, I believe my mom encouraged and supported me through the funeral the way a parent would a child, or as a woman does her good friend. Apparently my mother, as a spirit, was there for me. And she continues to give me her strength and courage. Since then there have been other times when I have asked her for support. Not only have I felt the calm and received clarity, but I've felt my mother touch me on my shoulders.

Betty's mother was there for her when she needed her the most. Our departed loved ones will continue to provide us with support and nurturing during difficult times. At the moment of my own mother's passing her loving touch gave me, a young 16-year-old girl, the courage to call all of my relatives and let them know her spirit had been freed from her cancer-ridden body.

When the physically dying experience afterlife visitations or visions they often try to explain to family, friends, and healthcare professionals what they have just seen. In describing their celestial journeys, they are letting remaining loved ones know that physical death does not mean the obliteration of the spirit. Dying is just the beginning of the journey to the next dimension. Physical death heralds the end of the trip to the afterlife. As a society we really do need to redefine the words *dying* and *death*.

In the following dream account a grieving daughter is able to understand that her mother will always love her.

My mom passed on just this year, two weeks short of her 70th birthday. She was a single mom and I'm an only child. She gave her all to me. I was and am still so very upset about her death. Mom lived with me and she really was my very best friend. Her health problems began when she had an operation. After that I knew her time with me would be short. Having this awareness was extremely upsetting to me, but we made the best of the time she had left.

Each month Mom became more fragile, but she rarely complained so I don't think I knew just how close to the end she was. Eventually she suffered a series of debilitating strokes and this left her unable to speak to me. Thankfully I was able to be at her bedside, comforting and loving her right up until she passed away.

Because I was so shaken up by first her strokes and then her passing, I completely forgot about a dream I'd had about my mom until after her funeral. I actually had this dream just a few days before she passed. In my dream I saw Mom in a very large building with tall Grecian columns. Large numbers of people dressed in white were trying to get through two gigantic doors. Right in front of me was my mother. I knew it was her because of the color of her hair and a certain style of hat she was wearing. Mom was rushing to get through the doors and this made it difficult for me to keep up with her. Once she made it to the doors, they opened and a very bright light came streaming out. Once past the doors I saw that there were a lot of other people with her and that she was actually on an elevator. Everyone was dressed in white. She turned around and looked at me just as the doors closed.

I never realized this dream was her way of letting me know she was going to be okay. Since she couldn't talk to me before she died, this dream now makes sense. I finally realized this while I was picking up her ashes from the funeral home. It was her way of telling me she wasn't really leaving me.

Today, I really miss her, but because of this dream I'm convinced she's always with me. She was just concerned about me, as was her way, and she wanted me to know where she is.

I want to make several points about this particular departing vision. First, the bond this woman had with her mother was very strong. Again we see a relationship based on a lifetime of respect and love. When the mother experienced a severe stroke, she was unable to physically speak with her daughter. Trapped in a body that was no longer serving her must have left her feeling frustrated and powerless.

As her spirit began to separate from her paralyzed body, this mother was finally able to visit her daughter in a dream. She was able to let her daughter know she was alright, that she still loved her and would always be there for her.

The daughter was very distressed over her mother's stroke, so she was not in an emotional place to see the dream for what it was: a message of love and hope. Only after her mother physically passed was she able to truly understand the departing vision. As a result of this dream, both mother and daughter know they will forever be linked to one another.

I must also add that within this departing vision are common themes of an afterlife or heaven. The daughter says that in her dream everyone is dressed in white, and the Grecian columns are tall. During a departing vision, descriptions of heaven, the afterlife, or the next dimension are common. A colleague of mine said she was amazed as she listened to her physically dying aunt describe to the family at the bedside visions of heaven. Her descriptions of the afterlife brought the grieving family a sense of peace. Knowing who will be greeting our departing loved ones and where they are going is very reassuring.

As I have said, physical death doesn't end the relationship. But we do need to grieve and mourn when our loved ones make the trip to the next life. Such a move creates challenges and changes how we will connect with dear ones. Mourning these changes is essential for our emotional wellbeing.

My grandfather Wills was my anchor. Though he lived in California, almost 2,000 miles from me, we were still very connected. Even when we didn't speak by phone, I could still feel our connection, and this brought us both great joy. Just knowing where he was and how he was doing gave me a sense of calm during troubled times. When he passed it was as if I'd lost a strong, secure Internet signal and had been knocked off the Web. I felt as though I'd lost my anchor in the universe.

But my connection to my grandfather had not vanished. The anchor of love had just moved. It was this change that I had to grieve. Mourning or the act of grieving emotionally cleared my psyche, and with this I was able to begin exploring how to reconnect with him. Once I tapped into his otherworldly "signal," security returned.

Finally, I'd like to share an incredible afterlife account involving my own young son, Joshua, and his grandfather.

When my father-in-law was getting ready to leave this life, my own 3-year-old son was visited by an angel with red hair. The angel told him he was taking his "Da" to the sky. For Joshua, this afterlife being presented himself as a red-headed kid named Damus, and came and went as he pleased. According to my son, one minute Damus was there and the next he'd disappear.

When I'd talk to Josh about how Damus could seemingly appear at will, my son would become exasperated with me. He thought I should know that disappearing and reappearing was as normal as ordering a hamburger and fries at the local fast-food joint. He was also confused as to why I couldn't see his heavenly friend and would become upset when I'd ask, "Where is Damus now?"

Damus continued to visit my son until his grandfather died. Once my father-in-law passed, Damus never returned. With some research we eventually found out Damus was an Aramaic word for the Angel of Death. Neither my husband nor I had ever heard the name Damus before, and my 3-year-old son certainly would not have heard about Damus from his coloring books!

The departing vision shows us our connectedness with physically deceased loved ones is still out there. The location changes but the relationship continues. Love transcends physical death, and though the signal varies, the connection lasts through infinity.

Furthermore, without Steve Jobs's incredible foresight into alternate realities and multiverses, I don't think I would ever have been able to fully understand the notion of an afterlife. Happy travels Mr. Jobs, and thank you!

CHAPTER 9

Receiving Comfort from the Dead

Each friend represents a world in us, a world possibly not born until they arrive, and it is only by this meeting that a new world is born.

—Anaïs Nin

We ended the last chapter talking about what heaven or the afterlife might look like. Many of those who have shared their departing visions with me have also provided amazing descriptions of the next dimension. One theme reappears over and over: I've been told the clothing we will wear in the next life will "shimmer," "be white in color," or be "luminous."

Here is a historical departing vision in which detailed references are made to just this subject. In 1854 a mother is sitting with her ill daughter Daisy. She has grasped her hand. The 10-year-old child is about to pass, just seven months after her little brother Allie died. As this mother watches her second child leave this dimension for the next, she is surprised when she learns her son Allie is visiting her beloved daughter. Notice the detail Daisy provides to her mother and father about her brother. What people are wearing in the afterlife was a major focus of this heavenly encounter.

"Dear mamma, I do wish you could see Allie; he is standing beside you." Wondering how she could be conversing with her brother, when I saw not the least sign of conversation, I said, "Daisy, how do you speak to Allie? I do not hear you nor see your lips move." She smilingly replied, "We just talk with our think." I then asked her further, "Daisy, how does Allie appear to you? Does he seem to wear clothes?" She answered, "Oh, no, not clothes such as we wear. There seems to be about him a white, beautiful something, so fine and thin and glistening, and oh, so white, and yet there is not a fold, or a sign of thread in it, so it cannot be cloth. But makes him look so lovely."

The morning of the day she died she asked me to let her have a small mirror. I hesitated, thinking the sight of her emaciated face would be a shock to her. But her father, sitting by her, remarked, "Let her look at her poor little face if she wants to." So I gave it to her. Taking the glass in her two hands, she looked at her image for a time, calmly and sadly. At length she said, "This body of mine is about worn out. It is like that old dress of mamma's hanging there in the closet. She doesn't wear it anymore, and I won't wear my body anymore, because I have a new spiritual body which will take its place. Indeed, I have it now, for it is with my spiritual eyes I see the heavenly world while my body is still here. You will lay my body in the grave because I will not need it again. It was made for my life here, and now my life here is at an end, and this poor body will be laid away, and I shall have a beautiful body like Allie's."[1]

With this historical account, we again witness the dying comforting the living by sharing what the afterlife will be like. The little girl's brother has come to help escort her to the other side, another example of how we don't die alone. Finally, the brother's heavenly clothing is white in color, and the little girl knows once she sheds her tired body, she too will receive a spiritual wardrobe just like her brother's.

This account reminds us that centuries ago death and dying wasn't hidden away. Children weren't whisked off and sheltered from this life cycle experience. In my investigations I've found there have been physicians who were willing to accept departing visions as a sign of things to come. In the following 1878 account a woman shares a departing vision with her doctor, and he tells her this is a premonition of an upcoming death.

Toward the end of March, 1878, in the middle of the night and at a time when I considered myself awake, I thought I saw the door near the head of my bed open, and a white form come in, which grazed the head of the bed as it passed, came to a halt at its foot, and stood before me; this allowed me to see that its head and body were enveloped in white veils. Suddenly, lifting its hand, the form withdrew the veils which hid its face, and I was able to distinguish the features of my sister, who had been ill for some time in that very house. I called to her, crying out her name, and I saw her vanish instantly.

The following day, a little disturbed by this occurrence, I called Dr. Jenner into consultation, whose diagnosis was that my sister had only a few days to live. And, indeed, so it was.

I enjoyed perfect health, and was not prey to anxiety of any kind. My sister was in the care of our regular physician, who had suspected nothing serious in the illness, so that I had not been disturbed, or my sister either. Apart from these singular observations, I have never had a vision of any sort.[2]

This tale from 1878 is remarkable for several reasons. The experiencer, Ms. Romanes, has an unusual departing vision involving her sister—who is still alive. Concerned about the vision and fearing she herself is ill, Ms. Romanes then contacts her family doctor. Dr. Jenner tells her she is not ill, but that she's had a premonition of her sister's upcoming death. Shortly after this her dear sister does pass.

I can't imagine many modern-day doctors would be willing to give a diagnosis of this nature. Today's physicians would most likely make a referral to a psychiatrist or pull out the prescription pad for several powerful drugs! Also, again, notice in the vision the color used to describe the sister's garments was white, just as was Daisy's brother.

Similar to this historical account is the following modern-day departing vision. In this 2009 example from Finland, a departing soul receives assistance from the next dimension.

> There was a friend of mine, who, before she died, spoke many times with her brother who had been dead for five years. I have been writing about this matter and have interviewed the nurses here in our local hospice. Their experiences are much the same as they are all over the world.

Once again, family living in the afterlife provides guidance to a dear one as she begins to separate from the physical body and travel to her new celestial home. These experiences are universal. Similar to healthcare workers in the United States, this individual from Finland has discovered that nurses at her local hospice are having the same encounters. I've worked with several hospice workers, and one shared this with me: "When patients have these visions, I'll see them reaching out in front of themselves, almost trying to hug someone. In other instances they will start talking to people who aren't in the room and on down the line I'll learn the names they are calling out belong to deceased relatives."

Departing visions take the fear out of death for the dying. When the dying finally understand that physical death isn't the end, any apprehension they might have had about letting go and moving on is removed. Once they're at peace, their attention then turns to those who will be left behind. Feeling a renewed sense of tranquility about the journey ahead, the dying will work at comforting their loved ones. Caretaking continues in spite of the dying process.

SHARING TRAVEL PLANS

In this next modern-day departing vision, a grandmother comforts her adult children and granddaughter before she leaves her earthly body.

I'm not afraid to die because I know someone will come back to take you home. My grandmother's story was the best. She was getting ready to pass so she called all her children together. One of my relatives traveled several hours to be there. Just my grandmother's children were in the room with her before she died, and what she said to them was never mentioned. When they came out of her room, after she was gone, they were all stunned. The story they told us was that my grandmother told them what she wanted them to know and then she looked past them toward the door to her room and said, "Momma?" After that everyone turned and looked at the closed door, saw no one, and when they turned back, she was gone.

This grandmother waited for all of her adult children to arrive before passing on. She wasn't about to go until she shared with them one last lesson about life and death. The nurturer in her was still caretaking to the very end. Love continues even as physical death approaches. Once she had said what it was she needed to say, she was ready to take the spirit hand of her own mother and leave her aged physical body behind.

When family members witness departing visions together, they then have a cherished memory to discuss with one another after physical death has occurred. Such experiences bring people closer together. Those preparing to cross from this life to the other side can express their love for family and friends by openly talking about their departing visions. In sharing their travel plans they offer comfort to those left behind.

Recently I made a trip to Eastern Europe. I knew communication with my family would be very difficult and that extra effort would be needed to contact them. To ease their fears I first described in detail those people who would be helping me get to my destination. I then told my two sons what I knew about Eastern Europe. Showing them pictures of my hotel gave them an idea of where I'd be staying. I also found Internet cafes in the towns I'd be visiting and told them they would hear from me by video mail. Just before I boarded the airplane departing for Poland and Belarus, I telephoned them again to let them know just how much I loved them. Then I reassured my guys I'd be seeing them soon. I was getting ready to go on a great adventure, but I knew I needed to take care of my family before I left.

Our dying loved ones will often do exactly the same thing. They recognize there is a great adventure before them, with caring friends and family on the other side to assist them in their journey, but this doesn't minimize concern for family and friends left behind. Just because someone is dying doesn't mean love and care stops.

HOLDING BACK

Those preparing for an afterlife trip often want to tell us where they are going and who will be helping them get there. The only reason the dying wouldn't share their departing visions with us is (a) if they are unprepared for their own departing visions and these visitations take them by surprise, (b) if they are fearful that sharing these extraordinary accounts will frighten us, or (c) if they are concerned they will be ridiculed or over-medicated and told they are just having hallucinations.

When the dying sense we are uncomfortable hearing what it is they have to say, they will refrain from sharing. For example, in 1906 a lawyer in Italy, Gaëtan Rè David, who appeared to be in good health, tried to tell a priest he had experienced a departing vision. Unfortunately, the priest would not take him seriously!

"The conversation turned on...communications with the deceased.... Whilst he was speaking of this as a matter of but slight interest, M. Rè David paused as if arrested by a surprising thought and said to me: 'Listen, Professor [the priest was also a professor], my mother died forty-one years ago and I have never dreamed of her. But last night she appeared to me in a dream, and she came towards me with open arms; I too opened my arms and we hugged and embraced each other. This dream awakened in me a conviction that my mother is calling me and that my death is near, very near. What do you say to that, Professor?'

'Dreams!' I replied.

However, three or four days later he was dead. The fact cannot fail to astonish...."[3]

After 41 years a loving mother came to escort her son to the afterlife. The son wanted to discuss this visitation with his priest, but the religious man dismissed him. What does this say about the priest? Chances are he was frightened by what he heard and didn't know how to respond.

Today, negative perceptions about afterlife contact continue. This way of thinking has forced many departing-vision experiencers into a closet of secrecy, confusion, and even shame. It's often not safe to discuss afterlife encounters openly in traditional settings. Fear of ridicule from the medical and even religious communities continues to silence not only experiencers, but also those seekers who are in grief over a recent physical death.

Luckily, the woman in the next modern-day example had information about departing visions that helped her withstand misguided comments from a healthcare worker.

When my friend was close to passing, a retired nurse who had worked with her stopped by to see how she was doing. I started telling this retired nurse that my friend had lain in bed that day saying

"Mother," and then "Daddy," with her eyes closed and a very distraught look on her face. She was kind of whimpering as she said "Mother" and then "Daddy." When she was talking to her parents, the look on her face was as if she wanted to cry.

Well, the retired nurse said to me, "She's just dreaming," and that was the end of that conversation. Thankfully, I knew better than that. I knew that her mother and daddy were there with her, and I also knew her death would come soon.

It did, and in fact it was about four days after this that she did pass away.

I have done a lot of reading on these sorts of experiences. What surprised me was that this retired RN who had worked all her life with hospital patients was sitting there telling me, "She's just dreaming." Wouldn't you think healthcare workers *know* when a dying patient is meeting their parents who are already deceased? And to further aggravate me about this situation, this retired nurse had also been a close friend of the deceased parents for years!

Though many experiencers keep silent, statistics tell a different story. According to a recent Gallop poll, at least 32 percent of the population believes the spirits of the deceased can come back in certain places or situations, and 21 percent believe people can mentally communicate with someone who has died.[4]

What this means is that out of more than 300 million people in the United States, around 100 million citizens admit to believing the spirits of the deceased can return to the earth plane. Along with this, almost 66 million of us believe the dead can communicate with us. Those seekers looking for answers explaining afterlife encounters make up almost one third of the U.S. population. For these individuals, manufactured or sensationalized television examples of spirit contact isn't going to be enough.

If you are part of the population who has experienced contact and is now looking for answers, hopefully you are beginning to feel supported. If you are a seeker who hasn't yet had an afterlife encounter, but wants more proof of life after death, read on. In the next chapter the presented experiencers have actually seen "something" leave the body as physical death approaches. Visually witnessing such marvels leaves us truly believing death isn't the end of the journey. Dying is having one foot in this world and the other in the next. Death is really just about having both of our spiritual feet planted in the afterlife.

CHAPTER 10

The Light After Life: Is This the Soul?

Our spirits are like birds confined in cages. Their cage doors have been set open—ours are still shut. But we can hold communion through the bars.

—Florence Marryat

After reviewing many afterlife accounts from across the United States, Australia, Germany, Scotland, South America, Portugal, Israel, Jamaica, England, Thailand, Russia, Finland, Italy, China, Portugal, Ireland, Poland, Brazil, South Africa, Wales, Denmark, and more, I know our deceased loved ones visit us. When they appear they look healthy and well. At other times they will come to us as white orbs of energy or shimmering forms of light.

We've discussed the possibility that heaven is just another dimension, and when we physically die our consciousness or soul disentangles itself from our material body in order to make the trip to this next level of existence. The question is, has anyone ever witnessed this separation? Who has seen the soul outside the physical body?

In the American Standard Version of the Holy Bible, in the book of James, Chapter 4, Verse 14, we read, "What is your life?" All of us have asked ourselves this question. Surprisingly, this statement is followed by, "For ye are a vapor, that appeareth for a little time, and then vanisheth away." When I first read this I almost fell out of my chair! Why, you might ask? Because I have seen this "vapor."

Hardcore scientists tell us we are nothing more than firing brain cells, genetics, and hormones, and are a product of evolution, but I don't believe this for one second. In 1997, I spent time in the home of famed near-death-experience researcher and best-selling author Dr. Raymond Moody. During my visit, I made visual contact with all of my deceased loved ones who had passed on to the next dimension. When they came to me, they did so as orbs of brilliant bluish-white light.

I accomplished this with the help of an ancient technique called "mirror gazing." In ancient Greece, reflective objects or surfaces, such as mirrors, fresh water springs, still pools of water, and bowls of liquid, were considered gateways to the spiritual world. I'd been invited by the famed researcher to join a team of other investigators to explore the early practice of mirror gazing using a "psychomanteum." Moody's psychomanteums were blacked-out rooms containing one large mirror.

Following is my incredible experience within the psychomanteum. The account comes from my book, *A Glimpse of Heaven: The Remarkable World of Spiritually Transformative Experiences*. I had met Moody in the early 1990s, at the height of his involvement with the psychomanteum. He invited me to come to his home to investigate current-day mirror-gazing practices. Though I was extremely skeptical and did not have a great deal of faith in this ancient device, I decided to take him up on his offer. The following is a letter I wrote to a friend of mine, just days after my return home.

Though words can never fully describe my experience, I will try to explain to you what I encountered. When I arrived at Moody's, I immediately learned that on the previous night a professional woman, who had recently lost her husband, had had an interesting experience in the psychomanteum. She had made contact with her father, who had passed 30 years ago, and saw him in solid form. He told her to quit worrying about her husband, that he was just fine. Even after hearing her riveting account, I had decided I wasn't going to be having any profound experiences that weekend.

Three psychomonteums were set up around Moody's eccentric, 100-year-old house. Within these devices, one of which had been built into the house, the walls are completely black. Along with this, there is a mirror hanging on the wall at one end, while at the other, facing the mirror, is a chair. That's it!

During the first day of my visit, I spent about 30 minutes in two of the psychomonteums. Seated comfortably, I reflected on my relationships with those loved ones of mine who had passed, and, as I had predicted, nothing out of the ordinary happened. From a historical perspective I found the psychomonteums interesting, but eventually decided enough was enough and spent the rest of the day chatting with other guests.

That evening, I enjoyed a light supper with the rest of Moody's visitors and had a delightful time talking with Dianne Arcangel, who has spent years researching both ancient and modern-day psychomanteums.

While eating dessert, I suddenly had a strong desire to put my plate down and go upstairs to the third psychomanteum. I had not been in this one. What was funny about this sudden "urge" was that during dinner, I made fun of this particular psychomanteum, as a rather obsessive engineer had built it.

So, up the stairs I trudged, like a woman on a mission.

Into the black box I went and sat down. Within just a few minutes of mirror-gazing (just looking into a plain old mirror hanging on a wall, about 4 feet away), a mist, clouds, or blue-gray "something" started pouring out of the mirror. A swirl of mist touched me on my right wrist and I became frightened. At this point, Dianne Arcangel happened to be walking by, heard me gasp, and asked if she could help me. I responded with, "I'm glad you are there because it's getting weird in here. I don't know who's visiting, but there are many, and I'm feeling very overwhelmed!" Something intuitively told me I was encountering many visitors from the other side. Dianne asked me if I wanted to continue. Hearing her voice calmed me down, and I said yes.

After she left, I began saying to myself, "What can I learn from this?" over and over again. This mantra kept me grounded. Within moments, it was happening again. This time, the mirror first became black, and then light. After this, white light tinged in blue started sprinkling down upon me. I wasn't scared, and I could even hear Moody talking on the telephone in the next room. Then the sprinkle of light turned into balls of light. These balls of light started to get bigger, and it looked like they were trying to take form. One began to take the shape of a head, and I thought to myself, *I wonder if that is my grandmother...*

The next part of the experience is still hard to talk about. I get very emotional. One of these bluish-white orbs, not very large in size, hit me on my left side, near my heart area. Though it felt like a light push, it literally took my breath away. It was as if the light had gone through me. With this, I suddenly felt very peaceful, joyous, calm, and intensely loved. I also noticed the temperature in the psychomanteum was suddenly cooler.

Then I saw more light around me and I was inundated with limitless unconditional love. Because it felt as though things were happening rather quickly, I sensed urgency for contact from whomever was reaching out to me. With this awareness, very thin etheric streams of whirling white energy come toward my left side, touching my left arm, as if in an embrace. From this soft, cool touch, I felt pure amazement and joy.

I will never know what would have happened next because one of Moody's more aggressive visitors suddenly burst in and told me he wanted to try this psychomanteum. With this intrusion, the swirling, loving light immediately disappeared. For a moment, I just sat there stunned. Then, in a state of awe, love, confusion, grief, and numbness, I got out of the psychomanteum and started to talk to the other guest about my experience, but then silenced myself. Outside the room, I once again found Dianne Arcangel. After seeing the look on my face, she led me to on outside porch where I began to cry. The encounter had overwhelmed me and I now found myself missing the loving touch I had received from the cool, swirling, whitish-blue light.

Out of a group of approximately 10 or so participants, I was one of two who experienced a reunion. My rational mind wants to explain the experience away, but it can't. I saw with my eyes and tactilely felt something beyond this physical plane of existence. During the encounter my intuition was certain, unshakable. The outpouring of gray misty clouds that initially floated toward me, the whitish-blue balls or orbs of soft, love energy and light that entered me, the unexpected drop in temperature inside the psychomanteum, and the streams of pure white, swirling, thin light energy that came toward me, encircling me, cannot be explained away. I am changed forever.

When I have shared this dramatic experience with skeptics, I am met with a number of questions such as, "Had you been drinking?" "Were you on drugs?" "Was the mirror rigged?" "Who was flashing a flashlight at you?" and "Were you psychologically stressed at the time?"

"I don't drink, nor do I do drugs, and I'm boringly sane," is the response I typically begin with. Having examined the mirrors hanging in the psychomanteum, I can attest to the fact that there were no secret lights or hidden panels contained within them. They were typical mirrors.[1]

For years I didn't publicly share this account, and for good reason. Raymond Moody himself was committed to a mental hospital for erratic behavior by his father, a well-respected physician, shortly after he talked to him about his work with the psychomanteum (Moody discusses this in his book *Paranormal: My Life in Pursuit of the Afterlife* [2012]). Moody's mood swings were later attributed to a thyroid condition, not his work with mirror-gazing in a psychomanteum. But being a visible self-help author, my fear of being discredited was very real. I didn't have the courage to go public until 2004.

Though I wasn't willing to talk openly, I knew my encounter wasn't unique. As a matter of fact, it prepared me for similar experiences to come. Let's take a look at the next account from my own life and see how it parallels the one we just reviewed.

On Friday, December 13, 1996, Dr. Sylvan Brandon died. He was born in Montpelier, France, to two physicians, but the family eventually returned to extended loved ones living in Russia. Sylvan followed in his parents' footsteps by graduating from the University of Wilno and becoming a physician himself.

While back in France courting my mother-in-law, out of curiosity he attended a Communist meeting. After the authorities discovered this, he was then told to leave France with his wife in 1938. This "young man" mistake would prove to be the couple's saving grace. The couple decided to immigrate to the United States and live with an uncle. Shortly after immigrating in 1938, the remaining family in Russia and Europe faced the horrors of Hitler and the abuses of Stalin.

My father-in-law was one of those vivacious individuals who lived life with gusto. As a medic in the army he witnessed the terror of World War II. Throughout the rest of his life Sylvan never forgot just how lucky he was to be a citizen of the United States.

When Sylvan was passing, my husband, Michael, would spend his nights at his father's bedside. The two were very close. To this day I still get tears in my eyes remembering the devotion son and father had for one another. One morning, Michael returned home to shower and dress for work, but instead of looking depressed and exhausted, he was upbeat and cheery. Quickly climbing the stairs of our hundred-year-old house I heard him call out with excitement, "Carla!" At first I thought Pop had moved on, but when I saw my husband I knew something else was up. Standing in the doorway of our bedroom he began describing a unique departing vision.

"It was dawn and I'd been asleep. I woke up and was getting ready to come home when suddenly I saw this colorful, swirling mist leaving Pop's body, near his chest area. At first I thought I was imagining this but as I sat there looking in shock, it continued. It was sparkling and full of pastel-type colors. The colors were amazing."

When my husband had this vision, I'd been actively investigating departing visions for just more than 15 years. Outside of his experience and my own in the psychomanteum, I hadn't heard very many firsthand accounts similar to this. After Pop passed, I mentioned this encounter to one of my husband's relatives. She looked at me with surprise, and then said, "I saw the same thing when my mother passed." In 2001 the *Houston Chronicle* interviewed me for an article titled "Departed Loved Ones Coming Back to Say Goodbye," and I suggested they include my husband's cousin's account too. Here is an excerpt from that article.

An only child, Hess had been terrified when her mother was diagnosed with leukemia more than 10 years ago.

Her fear grew a few months later when her mother suffered a heart attack as paramedics prepared to take her to the hospital for further treatment.

Hess was sitting on a nearby sofa with her father when it happened. "I'd never experienced anything like this, but I physically saw her spirit leave," she said. "It hovered over where Dad and I were sitting, and I just had this incredible feeling of peace. I knew everything would be okay."

Hess grieved when her mother was pronounced dead later that day, but she also took strength from what she had seen.

"What it let me know was that I didn't have to let go," said Hess, 47, a middle school art teacher in Clear Lake. "The loss I thought would be there really wasn't. Yeah, I missed the day-to-day conversations, and I still do after 10 years. But it erased so many fears in one fell swoop."

Still, she didn't tell anyone for years. Not even her father.

It was too personal. Too emotional. When she did finally begin to share her story, she discovered that she wasn't alone, but people were hesitant to talk about their own experiences.[2]

With these powerful family experiences, I thought I'd better start digging into historical deathbed vision literature for answers. Returning to Sir William Barrett's research, I again found validation.

In a letter that has recently been sent to me of a late well-known dignitary of the church (a Dean) in New South Wales, he describes the death of his son a few years ago.

He says at about 3:30 p.m. he and his wife were standing one on each side of the bed and bending over their dying son, when just as his breathing ceased they both saw "something rise as it were from his face like a delicate veil or mist and slowly pass away." He adds, "We were deeply impressed," and remarked, "How wonderful! Surely that must be the departure of his spirit. We were not at all distracted so as to be mistaken in what we saw."[3]

Barrett's account is similar to what my cousin had described. The soul, spirit, or consciousness appears to be escaping a sick, collapsing physical body. Was this mist the true essence of the dying person? Intrigued, I went looking for more similar accounts and found that popular American novelist Louisa May Alcott also witnessed a similar departing vision.

Born in Germantown, Pennsylvania, in 1832, Alcott published more than 30 books in her life. As for most young girls of my generation, Alcott's popular book *Little Women* was required school reading—and was also a favorite of mine. The main character of the story, Jo March, was actually based on Alcott's own youth. A feisty tomboy, the soon-to-be author enjoyed playing the parts of villains when she and her beloved sisters acted out dramas for friends.

Alcott's character Jo March gave me permission to climb trees, build forts, and race the boys on my bicycle. Like Jo March, Alcott was also very close to her sisters, so when death struck one of her siblings, Alcott was at her side.

The following is an excerpt from the life, letters, and journals of Louise May Alcott.

August (1857)—A sad anxious month. Betty [sister] worse; Mother takes her to the seashore.

September—Mother in Boston with poor Betty who is failing fast.

October—Find dear Betty a shadow, but sweet and patient always. Fit up a nice room for her, and hope home and love and care may keep her.

November—Lizzie seems better, and we have some plays.

Twenty-five this month. I feel my quarter of a century rather heavy on my shoulders just now. I lead two lives. One seems gay with plays, etc., the other very sad,—in Betty's room; for though she wishes us to act, and loves to see us get ready, the shadow is there, and Mother and I see it. Betty loves to have me with her; and I am with her at night, for Mother needs rest. Betty says she feels "strong " when I am near. So glad to be of use.

January, 1858—Lizzie much worse; Dr G. says there is no hope. A hard thing to hear; but if she is only to suffer, I pray she may go soon. She was glad to know she was to "get well," as she called it, and we tried to bear it bravely for her sake.

Anna took the house-keeping, so that Mother and I could devote ourselves to her. Sad, quiet days in her room, and strange nights keeping up the fire and watching the dear little shadow try to while away the long, sleepless hours without troubling me. She sews, reads, sings softly, and lies looking at the fire,—so sweet and patient and so worn, my heart Is broken to see the change. I wrote some lines one night on "Our Angel in the House." (Jo and Beth [of "Little Women"]—L. M. A.)

February—A mild month; Betty very comfortable, and we hope a little.

Dear Betty is slipping away, and every hour is too precious to waste.

Lizzie makes little things, and drops them out of windows to the school-children, smiling to see their surprise. In the night she tells me to be Mrs. Gamp, when I give her lunch, and tries to be gay that I may keep up. Dear little saint! I shall be better all my life for these sad hours with you.

March 14th. My dear Beth died at three this morning, after two years of patient pain. Last week she put her work away, saying the needle was "too heavy," and having given us her few possessions, made ready for the parting in her own simple, quiet way. For two days she suffered much, begging for ether, though its effect was gone. Tuesday she lay in Father's arms and called us around her, smiling contentedly as she said, "All here!" I think she bid us good-bye then, as she held our hands and kissed us tenderly. Saturday she slept, and at midnight became unconscious, quietly breathing her life away 'til 3; then, with one last look of the beautiful eyes, she was gone.

A curious thing happened, and I will tell it here, for Dr. G. said it was a fact. A few moments after the last breath came, as Mother and I sat silently watching the shadow fall on the dear little face, I saw a light mist rise from the body, and float up and vanish in the air. Mother's eyes followed mine, and when I said, "What did you see?" she described the same light mist. Dr. G. said it was the life departing visibly.[4]

The doctor comforts the author and her mother by telling them the mist is life departing the physical body. The physician appears to have no need to discount the experience or suggest medication for Alcott and her mother. In validating the account, the good doctor became part of the solution as opposed to adding to their grief. How many medical workers today would make a statement like this?

In this next account a nurse is sitting with a dying man when suddenly she witnesses an event that will stay with her for a lifetime.

> [S]urrendering his last breath I saw a beautiful silvery and blue light..., If I had blinked I would have missed it.... [I]t was his soul, his spirit exiting his body.... I have seen the spirit leave the body many times since then and it takes my breath away every time.[5]

Wow! I suspect many of us hope and pray a nurse such as this will be by the bedside of our dying loved ones. Being blessed with a healthcare professional like this is uncommon, but not unheard-of.

The next account comes from the collection of my friend Doc Dave. Here we see again something leaving at the moment of passing, but this time the words *white wisp* are used.

> About three years ago, working as a nurse..., I watched a lady die from cancer. A white "wisp" came out of her forehead. It looked like a tiny white tornado to me. I looked at the other nurse and I said, "Did you see that?" She just asked me, "See what?"

> I know she didn't [see it] but it got me thinking that I just saw the soul leave the body, so now, every time I see someone die, which is a lot because I work in nursing homes, I look for the "soul." I have seen it again a few times; sometimes it's a spark,

and sometimes it's just a sluggish white form. I *know* that it *has* to be the soul because immediately after I see it, the person takes his or her last breath, maybe one more reflex breath, but it's always right after I see it.

I've thought about taking a picture of it, but I wouldn't know how to, and sometimes the family is in the room, and that wouldn't be possible. Most of the time though, it's us nurses that are there with them. I find that a dim room is the best and to just look right at the forehead. In a second you'd miss it. I hope this helps you believe in the soul, I really think God lets me see this because my search for ghosts and contact with the other world is my way of finding "proof" that there is life after death. I just want to know we are here for a reason, and when we die, we just don't die and rot. The soul goes on! [6]

This healthcare professional is very clear that the white wisp she saw was the soul. These powerful experiences leave an indelible imprint on our consciousness. We know for a fact that what we've just witnessed cannot be explained away as a hallucination.

In the next incredible account we have an entire team of healthcare professionals in a surgical setting witness something phenomenal as their patient dies.

Stockholm—A team of surgeons, struggling feverishly in a futile effort to save the life of a plane crash victim watched in stunned amazement as the man's soul departed his lifeless body!

The incredible drama which offers irrefutable proof of life after death unfolded in a Swedish hospital.

And the vapor-like specter that rose from the victim's mangled body was seen by three famous surgeons, an anesthesiologist, six nurses, and four technicians.

"Everything happened so suddenly and quickly that I sometimes wonder if I just imagined it," Dr. Jan Lundquist, the anesthesiologist, told reporters.

"But I didn't just imagine it. We all saw it—a dazzling misty-blue light that came right out of the body. It floated upward and then just seemed to dissolve like a stream into nothing. I wasn't surprised at all that the patient died. He was in a terrible state. The surgeons did everything they could. But even as they worked, I knew we were losing him. Suddenly every vital sign ceased. All life signs just stopped. There was just a deep, hollow, moaning sound and I looked up to tell the surgeon that our patient was gone. That's when I saw an incredible shimmering light. Right before our eyes that glowing vapor rose. Somehow I was watching the soul leave the mortal remains of the man who lay before me."

Dr. Ulta Jurgenson, one of the three surgeons who also witnessed the miracle, said she tried to find some other explanation for what she saw. But she said she is now convinced the misty phantom that rose before her eyes could only have been the dead man's soul.

"I have been an atheist all my adult life," the 53-year-old surgeon said. "I have never believed in God or the hereafter. But now I'm not so sure. All I know is that I saw something that I cannot explain rise up out of the body of a dead man."[7]

For those of us who have witnessed a departing vision, we know we are changed forever. Experiencing any sort of afterlife encounter can tear down any misconceptions we have about the continuation of life. Such experiences force us to reevaluate not only our spiritual beliefs, but also every aspect of our lives. We now have a new paradigm for living life. Materialism takes a backseat to deeds of service and further spiritual exploration.

The medical professionals in Stockholm who watched this misty blue light float over the body of their dying patient were greatly affected by this event. I'm sure they spent months trying to understand what they witnessed, and also reflecting on life, death, and their place in the universe. The departing vision experience redefines who we are and what life is all about. Such events can take up to a year to integrate into our everyday living experience.

Leaving Sweden and returning to the States, in the next account we have a departing vision discussing a blue "cloud."

It was during the last 36 hours of my mother-in-law's life that I witnessed this Spirit-Soul differentiation. Approximately a day and a half prior to Roselyn's death, it became apparent that she was struggling in her death process. A friend and I decided to pray for her wellbeing, without attaching to the appearance of it. As my friend and I held hands across Roselyn's bed, we began to pray, and as we prayed we could sense a great release, or a feeling of peace. As we continued in prayer, I saw a medium-blue cloudy essence, Roselyn's soul, leave her body. It emerged through the soles of her feet, and funneled up through the bridge we had created over her body with our outstretched arms....

[The next evening Roslyn passed.][8]

I love this account. Did you notice how the daughter-in-law and her friend prayed for Roselyn's spiritual well being? They didn't ask that she be cured or to not physically die. Instead, they turned her over to a Higher Power. If we pray over dying loved ones and ask that they stay with us, if they really need to move on we will not be helping them. This actually makes physical passing more difficult. What Cynthia did wasn't easy, but it was the loving thing to do. My personal prayer in situations like this is, "Thy will be done."

As we continue to explore the soul leaving the body let's look at two more departing visions. They come from my friend Brad Steiger's book, *Real Ghosts, Restless Spirits, and Haunted Places.*

Bill W. told Palmer that he saw the spirit of his brother as it disengaged from the dying body. The cloud-like vapor took on human shape, clapped its hands in joy, and passed upward through the ceiling in the company of an angel.[9]

Jerry C. of Denver, Colorado, stated that when his 10-year-old son died, he saw the child's spirit leave the body as a luminous cloud and rise upward toward the ceiling.[10]

Did you notice how similar the accounts are? The word *cloud* was used by both experiencers.

In 2005 I received an amazing departing vision from another brave soul who had gone public with his experiences. Scott Degenhardt worked on spacecraft for NASA and spent some years on a laser research project at Vanderbilt University's Free-Electron Laser Center. In other words, this is one smart cookie! He contacted me after completing his first book, titled, *Surviving Death*. Scott specifically wanted me to see the chapter he had dedicated to his father. Because this departing vision account is so powerful, I encourage you to follow up and read his book in its entirety. Thank you, Scott, for your wonderful contribution!

It wasn't the end, it was the beginning. I witnessed the start of forever. Here, in explicit detail, is the story of my encounter with my father after he "died," left his body, and headed to his next mission....

The last time I saw my father alive, they were sucking fluids from his lungs through a tube. I had said my goodbye the day he slipped into a coma. I never expected to see my father again until the funeral. On the night of May 29, my father had been in a coma for a day and a half. It was around 11 p.m. I lay in bed mulling over the past few days. I was trying to mentally prepare myself for "the call."

After about an hour, I managed to drift to sleep from pure mental exhaustion. It was around this time, shortly after midnight, that I was awakened—by my father!

I was startled awake by a white vapor that whooshed above where I lay and hovered at my left shoulder. Words are inadequate to describe what happened next, but I will do my best to paint the complete picture.

Somehow, a line of communication was established between my father and me—one that involved more than the five senses. I knew immediately, without a doubt, that this was my father. I knew because, when he entered the room, he was "radiating" who he was...his true soul, his true essence.

The last bit of ID he radiated was that of, "I was just released from my physical body, and boy, do I feel better than I can find words to describe!" This gave me the clue that he must have just died. In fact, I knew he had just died. I could feel the freshness of his having just left his body, like a genie out of a bottle, finally released from eternal servitude to the "master" of the physical body. I could feel his transitional experience of leaving the physical plane as he was feeling it. I could feel my father...as if I were my father. Not only did I feel my emotions, but

I felt his emotions, too. And we were both basking in bliss—over the top, emotionally!

My father had the appearance of being younger, perhaps in his early 30s. He was "himself" from the waist up—having a torso, arms, neck, head, and face. But from the waist down his white, misty, vaporous body tapered off to sort of a point. His face: he had a huge smile on his face!

...He was feeling better than is possible on this earthly plane! ...Then, above us, a porthole or tunnel opened to some distant realm. At the other end of the opening I could "hear" beings.... I did get the distinct impression that they were "overseers" or guides for my father, and possibly for me. I felt as if they were higher beings—what we might call angels.

These beings conversed among themselves and then they said something directly to my father.... With an incredible sense of new mission in his tone, he said, "They're calling me now, and I have to go." As he said this, I replied, "Great!"

With that, he whooshed off into the eternal distant land.

...the phone rang and woke me up. My mother answered it before I could. She came to my door a minute later, and said, "That was the hospital calling. Your dad just died."[11]

Though the skeptics would have us believe death is the end, this is false. Scott's account is a wonderful example of just how connected we remain to loved ones who have traveled to the next dimension. After packing up their "personality" along with all they have learned in this life, these dear ones leave their "organic wardrobe" behind, and begin the journey to the next adventure. The departed never abandon us and can even visit us. When our time to physically die comes, they will always be there for us.

Not long ago another reader of mine was relieved to learn other experiencers had seen the soul leave the body at the moment of death. She shared her most personal account with me; like Scott, she too saw a "mist."

> In 2004 my mother passed away, and before she died she had many deathbed visions... As she would tell me things, I knew right away that something out of the ordinary was going on.... I'd never heard of DBVs and wish I could have been more informed as I was witnessing these things.... I saw a white mist leave my mother's mouth several hours before she died.
>
> The experiences I've had with my mother's dying have been life-altering. I can't really discuss with a lot of people the things that happened or they would come with the butterfly net for sure.

This woman had an astonishing experience with her mother, but like so many of us she was then reluctant to share what she saw. Fear of being misunderstood and then ridiculed forced her to be cautious about being open with her account. Apprehension can silence us.

One day a woman named Lisa wrote to me about a similar experience she and her husband had—unlike the previous experience, they weren't about to stay quiet! When Lisa's mother passed over the couple experienced a powerful departing vision.

My mother unexpectedly died March 8th in the coronary care unit and I've had a hard time dealing with her death— until I read your book, *One Last Hug Before I Go.* I began the book last weekend and just finished it last night. I can't tell you how much that book has comforted me. I clung to each story, and wanted to share what my husband and I noticed during her passing. We both saw my mother look up and down a couple of times directly in front of her; then she died. At that time, my husband noticed a gray mist above her body for just a split second. He wasn't going to say anything, but when I asked him a week later if he noticed anything unusual, he told me that. It was amazing that I had also read similar instances in your book!

What's even more amazing (or at least as amazing) is that my husband took a picture of my mother in the bed earlier that morning with his palm pilot. He said he didn't know why he took it, but I'm so glad he did. While reading your book this past week, I read the section on the father who took photographs of his wife and son. When it stated that he saw images on the photographs, I ran downstairs to the computer and put in the disk which had my mother's picture, and even with the poor resolution,

I could see a bright outline of what appears to be an angel or what we perceive to look like Jesus on the side of my mother!! This was taken approximately three hours before she died. Now we are wondering if she was looking at this angel/Jesus in front of her prior to her passing.

My mother was a devout Catholic who prayed to Jesus, Mary, and the Saints regularly. When I called my husband (who is Jewish) to come down and look at [the picture], he was the first to say it looked like Jesus! It's amazing. I sent it to my sister and she pulled it up on her computer and noticed it, too. It's not too clear, but I also brought it to the priest who spoke with my mother in the room prior to her death that morning to see what he had to say. I hadn't finished your book and didn't yet realize that he is not supposed to discuss that. He told me as a representative of the church that he couldn't comment on the picture, but before I left him, he asked if he could have a copy of the picture! That told me that he saw something, too!

Anyway, I can't thank you enough, Carla. You've helped remove so much of the fear I have had about death, and I now know that the connection with my mom and others gone before me remains.

I just can't say enough about this account Lisa has so graciously shared with us. First, the mist or spirit is visually seen leaving and then is captured on film. This again validates our discussion. Something does leave the body when death draws near.

Secondly, I've reviewed numerous photographs like this. There are many so-called spirit pictures that have been Photoshopped, and are definitely fakes. But every once in a while a photograph that's difficult to explain crosses my desk. The experiencer has no investment in creating a hoax and often wants to remain anonymous. These pictures are all very similar, with only minute variations in the depiction of the vapor or mist caught leaving the body.

Third, clergy are often told by their superiors not to respond to questions dealing with the paranormal. Sadly, in refraining from commenting they can't validate such experiences or use these reported accounts to aid grieving survivors. In this particular situation, we again have an example of a professional who won't comment.

Do I blame the clergy for being so cautious? To some degree, yes, but as I said earlier, I understand such reluctance. As you will see in the next chapter, going public can bring out the skeptics.

CHAPTER 11

Going Public
Despite the Skeptics

A skeptic is a person who would ask God for his ID card.
—Edgar A. Shoaff

All of us have questions about life after death. Those of you who have picked up this book have done so for several very specific reasons. Many of you are grieving departed loved ones and are looking for reassurance. Some of you might be physically dying and you are struggling to make peace with this. Possibly you have had a departing vision or been with a dying loved one who was greeted by deceased family or friends on the other side. Though the encounter was amazing, you are fearful of talking about this. I totally understand. Whatever your reason is for exploring the departing vision, hopefully you have seen the phenomenon is real. Though *you* may be convinced there really is more to life after this life, what about the skeptics? Know that they will try to derail you!

After witnessing a mist departing from our physically dying loved ones, my family and I learned from history that this was nothing new, yet all of us were fearful of talking about it. Speaking openly about such things typically resulted in wisecracks or comments about stress-related hallucinations, a need for medications, or unresolved grief. Likewise, when I wrote my first few books on afterlife contact, even contributors were asking that I not give out their identities. Many of my readers who had shared their departing visions with me also refused to give me permission to publicly discuss their accounts. Coming forward takes courage, and though it isn't always easy, it is necessary. The next brave experiencer, a physician, shows us why such encounters should always be shared.

I entered Hazel's room wondering if today her tired and weary body would surrender to the mysterious unknown. She had been unconscious and unresponsive all the previous day and I expected she would die that night. Part of me was surprised to learn she was still alive....

Just as I was about to leave, Hazel sat bolt upright in bed. I was surprised and amazed. Lazarus-like, she had woken.... Her eyes however, were fixed directly ahead....

Something had brought Hazel to life and captured her attention. Something that was invisible to me and to the nurse who was with me. Having heard and read about these strange deathbed scenes I asked, "What can you see?" I placed myself in her line of sight and repeated the question. Hazel looked straight through me, engrossed and captivated by what she saw....

I am unsure how long it took—it seemed quite a while but was probably only a minute or two. Hazel then lay back on the pillow and then without a word or a sigh let go of life. [1]

This doctor displayed amazing awareness. Instead of over-medicating or brushing off Hazel's experience, he stayed with her until she had moved on.

The Skeptics Throw a Punch

In 2002 the Committee for the Scientific Investigation of Claims of the Paranormal (CSICOP, which recently changed its name to the more media-friendly Committee for Skeptical Inquiry, or CSI) tried to take a public jab at me after the release of my first book on the departing vision. Following is part of the relevant article "'Visitations': After-Death Contacts" in the *Skeptical Inquirer*'s Investigative Files (Volume 12.3, September 2002), by Joe Nickell.

Like others before her (e.g., Kubler-Ross 1973), Wills-Brandon promotes deathbed visions (DBVs) largely through anecdotal accounts which, as we have seen, are untrustworthy. She asserts that "the scientific community" has great difficulty explaining a type of DBV in which the dying supposedly see people they believe are among the living but who have actually died.[2]

It's perfectly appropriate and even necessary to question information we are reviewing, but when I first read this I just had to laugh. Instead of looking at the research I'd included from well-known scientifically trained clinicians, medical personnel, and university professors, CSICOP author Joe Nickell only focused on one brief historical departing vision from 1893! Yes, I did have a good chuckle.

There are organizations out there like CSI that are devoted to going to any lengths to publicly discount authors, researchers, and even experiencers who try to share information with the public on topics dealing with life after death. Many of these folks regularly appear on television or radio programs in an attempt to misinterpret afterlife research by personally attacking well-meaning researchers and experiencers. Some even make lucrative careers out of this. Challenging research is very important, but distracting from the presented information by hurling assaults on the personality of investigators and experiencers is something else.

Recently, the piece including my investigations into departing visions was again reposted by Nickell and company. Thankfully, I'm a bit more thick-skinned today. Having been poked at by a number of groups and media personalities with views similar to CSI's, I'm used to such tricks. Unfortunately, for the more private person, such public battering can be hurtful.

GOING PUBLIC NO MATTER WHAT THE SKEPTICS SAY

In spite of ridicule from naysayers, a number of experiencers and researchers *are* willing to go public with their afterlife encounters. One hospice worker even went so far as to take her story to the airwaves. For a number of years, Rev. Margaret Lemay worked as a hospice chaplain and spiritual counselor. When called to the bedside of the dying, she would provide loving assistance and comfort. She also educated family members and healthcare professionals on departing visions, near-death experiences, and afterlife communications.

Now self-employed, Margaret continues to provide end-of-life spiritual care and grief healing on a private basis. Along with this she was the host of the popular radio show "HeartShifts: The Journey of Your Infinite Spirit." Margaret truly is a blessing to all those she works with. As she so eloquently says, "My job is to help the dying and their families understand dying is nothing to be frightened of."

Professionally comforting those who are about to pass took on new meaning when she found herself caring for her own terminally ill mother. When I was a guest on her radio program she shared with me and her listeners a great departing vision. In doing so Margaret validated the fact that our personality traits continue beyond this dimension.

My mother passed from cancer in 2005. Throughout the last six weeks of her life I was fortunate to be able to be with her, helping with her daily care and with the decision making needed for her wellbeing. After five weeks Mom's condition deteriorated and her medical and physical needs were increasing. As a family we had little choice but to move her into a full-scale nursing facility where she could receive the round-the-clock attention she needed. This proved to be the best decision for everyone.

After the move we were all exhausted, including Mom. I lived eight hours away and had not been home in weeks. Knowing Mom was in good hands at the nursing facility, I took the opportunity to go home for a few days. Mom seemed relaxed when I told her I was leaving and I promised I'd call twice a day. The sentiment from the staff at the facility was that she still had two to three weeks at least. They too encouraged us all to take a break and get rested.

Packing up the car and my dog, Gizmo, I drove nonstop and arrived home early in the evening. I got caught up on home news, and then dragged myself to bed. Within an instant, I was asleep.

After being asleep for a while, I found I was in that awake-but-lucid-dreaming place where it's difficult to distinguish between the two—asleep or awake. My eyes seemed open and I felt pulled to look toward the end of my bed. When I did I saw my mother standing there.

I said, "Mom, what are you doing?" Without her actually speaking she told me I had to return to her bedside—she was nearly ready to go. I know I was irritated and said to her, "I will come back after I have rested. I'm so tired. Please just give me a few days. Please. I need to sleep." She was patient but persistent about my returning to her.

Upon waking the next morning, I vividly recalled the image of my mother standing at the end of my bed and couldn't shake the feeling that this so-called dream was an actual visit by my mother's spirit. I found myself asking, "Was my mom's message true? Was she much closer to passing than I originally thought the day before? Should I call my family, or will I be getting that call saying she had already gone?" I had received enough experience working in spiritual care in hospice to know that messages from our loved ones often arrive in dream form.

Though I really wanted to stay at home a few more days I briefly considered leaving right then to drive back. Then I shuddered inside and tried my best to put the entire episode away, placing my focus on the present with a hot shower and a cup of coffee.

In truth, the dream continued to nag at me. The two to three weeks I thought mom still had now felt way out of line with the dream.

About 11 a.m. my phone rang. It was my brother. "Margaret," he said. I held my breath. "You better come back here."

"Did something happen? Is Mom gone?" I bravely asked.

"No," he said, "but we all think you should get back here right away. She is having trouble breathing, she is restless, and the nurses say it won't be much longer."

"Really? But I just left yesterday and she seemed stable. We even talked on the phone." I tried to reason.

"All I can tell you is that it's all different now and we need you here." He said.

"Okay, I'm on my way. Call me if anything changes," I directed.

As I repacked the suitcase, trying to think clearly enough to remember what to pack, I looked over at my dog, Gizmo. He stared at the suitcase with his most annoyed look, then at me, and walked away. I said to him, "You're going too, so don't get comfy!"

In two hours the dog and I were back in the car on the highway making the eight-hour drive again.

Throughout the entire drive I kept feeling this unexplainable pulling on me, almost as if someone had tied a rope around my waist and was gently pulling me forward. As tired as I felt, some force of energy kept me alert.

When I finally arrived back to the nursing home it was about 9 p.m. and Mom was still alive. I sat next to her bed, held her hand, and let her know I was there. She opened her eyes and looked at me. I could see the relief in her that I had arrived.

My siblings and other family were also all with Mom, waiting for her passing. After several hours of waiting, I felt the need to take care of Gizmo. I'd dropped him off at Mom's house. Feeding and watering him seemed like a break I could live with.

The drive to Mom's house was only a few minutes away. It felt good to get out in the fresh air and be away from that intense energy back at the nursing home. My dog greeted me enthusiastically and I set about getting his dinner. Within moments my phone rang, and it was my sister-in-law.

"Margaret," she said, "something's happened."

"What is it?" I asked.

"Mom sat up straight in bed with her eyes open, arms outstretched, and tried to talk! Then she laid right back down! We all think she was trying to tell us something and she seemed afraid!" My sister-in-law seemed very upset.

"Oh brother," I replied. "She was just reaching for whoever was there to take her on, help her move on. This is classic behavior for such a moment."

"No, no, I don't think so," my sister-in-law said. "You weren't here. You didn't see her face."

"I don't need to see her face, but I will be right there," I replied.

Off again I went back to mom's bedside. She was barely breathing and I knew her spirit had left her body during my absence. I just chuckled to myself, while calming the family. *It figures she would rouse me out of bed, insistent that I return, drive the eight hours to be at her bedside, only to move on when I'm gone feeding the dog!* I thought.

I still laugh about that today.

Because Margaret trusted her intuition and experience, she was able to calm her family when her mother had a departing vision. She also openly discussed her heavenly encounters on her very public radio program. In sharing, Margaret gave her listeners permission to openly talk about their afterlife experiences.

THE MOTHER OF THE DEATH AND DYING MOVEMENT GOES PUBLIC

Author and lecturer Dr. Elisabeth Kubler-Ross (cited in the CSICOP article at the beginning of this chapter) is another experiencer who decided to go public. This world-famous researcher, who pulled the topic of death out of the closet, was my first introduction into the psychology of dying. By opening up discussion about the process of coming to terms with a terminal illness and bereavement, she gave investigators like me permission to speak more freely about the dying experience.

For decades this physician clinically observed the incurably ill. Based on her studies she then produced a multitude of professional articles and books. Kubler-Ross's research is now the foundation for palliative care (death and dying) in hospitals and hospice organizations around the globe.

During her early years she heard patients talk about departing visions, but like so many professionals, Kubler-Ross ignored such accounts. As time went on she began to recognize something was happening. Descriptions of otherworldly visions and visitations from the dying were very similar in nature from patient to patient, and this caught her attention. Intrigued, she started to document and collect the reported visions.

Kubler-Ross wrote her first book, titled *On Death and Dying*, in 1968. In the original manuscript she included an entire chapter devoted not just to the departing vision, but also to near-death experiences. Fearful she wouldn't be taken seriously, she removed the chapter before sending it off to her publisher. But this didn't mean Kubler-Ross wasn't a believer; she herself had been visited by a deceased patient of hers named Mrs. Schwartz.

Previous to physical death Mrs. Schwartz had experienced a near-death experience. She found herself up near the ceiling watching a resuscitation team work on her body below. She described in detail for her physician what had occurred and asked if she was psychotic. Kubler-Ross instead confirmed the woman's experience. This left the flustered Mrs. Schwartz feeling very relieved.

After her physical death, Mrs. Schwartz suddenly appeared to Kubler-Ross. Described as hovering in the air and almost transparent, Mrs. Schwartz thanked the doctor for her help. She then encouraged the researcher to continue her work on death and dying.[3]

Thankfully Kubler-Ross listened to Mrs. Schwartz. Aside from working with critically ill adults, she spent countless hours sitting at the bedsides of terminally ill or fatally injured children. While holding their small hands, she would wait patiently to see if they had anything to say. Departing visions were commonplace and she documented many of these incredible experiences in her 1992 book titled *On Children and Death*, as well as in *Death Is of Vital Importance: On Life, Death and the Afterlife*, published in 1995. One such account particularly caught my eye: A mother and her two sons were involved in a horrific car accident. The mother died instantly, but her two little boys survived and were taken to two separate hospitals. Kubler-Ross was attending one of the boys. This child had not been told his mother had passed. While attending her patient, the young boy, who had been in a coma, suddenly came to and said, "Everything is alright now. Mommy and Peter are already waiting for me..."[4]

The young child then smiled, and slipped back into a coma. Shortly after this he passed. As I said, Kubler-Ross knew the mother had died, but had no idea how the child's brother, Peter, was doing. "I was aware in this particular case that the mother had been killed immediately at the scene of the accident," Kubler-Ross said. "But I also knew that Peter had gone to a burn unit in a different hospital and that he, as far as I knew, was still alive. I didn't give it a second thought, but as I walked out of the intensive care unit by the nursing station, I had a telephone call from the hospital where Peter was. The nurse at the other end of the line said, "Dr. Ross, we just wanted to tell you that Peter died 10 minutes ago."[5]

With personal proof for the continuation of life after physical death, Kubler-Ross became even bolder. She eventually cared little about what people thought of her for speaking so freely about afterlife contact. Writing more than 20 books, she was bound and determined to get the word out. In going public, Kubler-Ross used her patients' remarkable deathbed visions and near-death experiences to show us that death is nothing to fear.

Here is what she had to say about the departing vision and those souls who escort us to the afterlife: "In general, the people who are waiting for us on the other side are the ones who loved us the most. You always meet those people first.... I never encountered a Protestant child who saw the Virgin Mary in his last minutes, yet she was perceived by many Catholic children. You are simply received by those who meant the most to you."[6]

Kubler-Ross had her critics, but during an interview in 1997 with the *San Francisco* Chronicle, she had this to say about the skeptics: "I only believe in what I see and hear with my own eyes and ears." (She experienced two of her own near-death experiences.) As for skeptics who claim these visions are mere hallucinations caused by a lack of oxygen to the brain, Kubler-Ross replies, "Let them wait until they experience it themselves."[7]

In 1995 Kubler-Ross suffered a massive stroke that paralyzed her left side. The chocolate-loving Swiss psychiatrist, who taught a generation how to begin talking about dying, suddenly found herself in great agony. She was ready to move on. Kubler-Ross even became angry with God, calling him a "procrastinator" for not letting her go. In 2004 her wish came true. The beloved researcher finally escaped her paralyzed, pain-ridden body for the freedom of the afterlife.

Elisabeth Kubler-Ross gave me the courage to brush off the skeptics when they challenged my work unfairly. This brave pioneer also paved the way for other credible modern-day researchers to step up to the public plate and openly share their own investigations and accounts. More medical doctors, nurses, hospice workers, scientists, media personalities, and mental healthcare professionals are also now coming forth with their own afterlife encounters, paving the road for the everyday experiencer.

Everyday People Just Like You Are Going Public

For many in society today the fear of dying is all-encompassing. When a loved one departs this world, overwhelming grief can disrupt every area of life. Aside from impacting relationships and spirituality, and intensifying the fear of death, the experience of just *living* becomes more difficult. Unresolved grief and loss turns into depression, intimacy phobia, and anger. Thankfully, this does not need to be our path.

Together, we have reviewed numerous, incredible departing visions from presidents, authors, theater people, researchers, and everyday people from around the world. The departing vision proves to us that in spite of physical death, relationships continue and we are never alone.

CONCLUSION

Where Do We Go from Here? Learning to See the Unseen

I go home!
—Peter Metzler *(After escaping the tyranny of Russia and immigrating to the United States, this distant relative of mine passed after a mishap on his uncle's farm in California. These were his parting words.)*

What was Peter Metzler talking about when he said, "I go home"? If we do indeed live in a universe that exists alongside other dimensions, do the souls of our loved ones travel to one of these worlds after physical death? Is this "home" just another dimension of existence?

My Mickey Mouse Theories

Many physicists believe numerous universes exist right alongside ours. Because these parallel worlds vibrate at much higher speeds they are invisible to the human eye. This concept was difficult for me to wrap my mind around. I needed some sort of earth-based analogy, and my childhood friend Mickey Mouse did the trick!

As a kid, I loved Saturday-morning cartoons. When I got older I even took a summer animation class. Sitting with my friends eating jelly beans, I learned how professional artists created incredible animations: A peg bar was used to hold the drawing of a cartoon character in place. Transparent paper was then laid on top of the original drawing. The drawing was copied, but not exactly; each frame was a little bit different. If the animator wanted to show a character throwing a ball, the first drawing would illustrate the ball in hand. The next two or four drawings might show the character preparing to throw the ball. With the final three frames we would see the ball being released from the hand.

Like most children, I created an animation of Mickey Mouse jumping up and down when I was in school. I had about 50 individual drawings in my three-second cartoon. When the drawings were shown in rapid succession the animation showed a continuous, smooth scene of Mickey leaping in the air. The individual frames were then difficult for the naked eye to identify. In slowing down the sequence, it became easier to see the differences in each frame.

I believe higher dimensions of existence operate a bit like a fast-moving animation.

Quantum physics has suggested that our world is denser and slower, and parallel universes are lighter and vibrate faster. Because of this, we can only catch a quick glimpse of these rapidly moving, lighter-density higher dimensions. In other words, while living in this world, seeing the detail of these heavenly universes will be difficult, if not impossible for many of us.

Witnessing the essence of our loved ones separate from the physical body as a mist, vapor, clouds, smoke, or silver encasements feels like a mystical encounter. In actuality, what's happening is that the departing soul's vibration is still moving slowly enough for the human eye to detect.

Those preparing to physically die begin to shake off the anchors binding them to their earthly bodies. With this release spiritual vibration begins to increase. As this vibration intensifies they not only see this world, but also a life to come. Looking toward heaven, the afterlife, deceased friends and relatives, and even angels, they are no longer afraid of physical death. They know where they are going and understand that the separation from dear family and friends is just an illusion.

When we are able to sense our deceased loved ones, either they have lowered their vibration level or we have somehow increased our own. I think it's that simple. If this is the case, how can we consciously raise our own vibration and build a solid bridge of contact with our loved ones living in the afterlife?

Increasing one's spiritual awareness takes work. We must first address any physical, emotional, or spiritual wounds hampering our progress. Addiction can also create problems. As my friend Buddy Stone says, "To be conscious you must be conscious." To avoid taking these first steps puts us at risk for remaining "stuck" in our own spiritual evolution.

HEALING PHYSICALLY AND EMOTIONALLY

In order to make contact with the afterlife, we must take responsibility for every area of our lives in this dimension. In starting my own journey it was imperative that I look within myself and explore what might be holding me back. In my case, the stumbling blocks were clear.

When my mother died, discussion about where her spirit had gone never happened. The "no talk" rule permeated my family. I responded to this by going to the pantry and grabbing a bottle of cheap red wine. Alcohol temporarily buried the pain of my mother's loss, but also kept me from grieving.

Before the funeral my grandmother pulled out a vial of white pills. After grinding up a couple of these tranquilizers she laced my grandfather's peanut butter sandwich with the drug, and also mixed it into orange juice. After serving this to me I found I was emotionally numb for most of my mother's service.

When it came time to close the lid on the silvery blue "Cadillac" casket, I decided to be brave and say goodbye. Making my way to the front of the funeral home, I saw a body that looked like my mother's...but something was missing. Confused, I again wondered where her spirit had gone.

Though I'd had a fantastic departing vision, the trauma of my mother's funeral, along with the pills and wine, kept me from healing from this loss. Not talking openly about death, dying, and the afterlife held me back spiritually.

Shortly after her physical passing, I discovered I was suffering from a debilitating medical condition. I had Crohn's disease. My choices for treatment were steroids, along with surgeries and drugs. I was addicted to alcohol and pain medications, and my emotions were frozen. I was cut off from my spirit.

START AT THE BEGINNING

When I was 28 years of age my mother had been gone for 12 years. One day while sitting on the beach I asked myself, "Is this how she would want me to live?" The answer was an immediate no. If I was to practice a spiritual life I had to start living a more balanced, holistic lifestyle. In 1984 I checked myself into a drug and alcohol center to cleanse myself of all of the medications and booze I'd become so addicted to. It wasn't easy, but with help I survived.

I also knew I'd never healed from a host of childhood traumas aside from my mother's passing. Hiding from my pain wasn't going to make it go away. Healing old wounds was going to be necessary for my spiritual growth. Thankfully, I found a good therapist who helped me with my grief work.

Trauma involving a troubled past, a lost love affair, a divorce, a major job change or geographical move, caring for aging parents, difficulty in raising children, experiences with war, a sexual assault, or any other number of intense life experiences can also block spiritual growth. Pushing this aside won't relieve us of the emotions associated with these events. Successfully raising our spiritual vibration can only happen if we are willing to clean up any emotional wreckage.

Unhealthy relationships can also block spiritual development. True intimacy and healthy connections with other likeminded people teaches us how to be spiritual beings. One-night stands and quick sexual interludes will leave us feeling empty and spiritually disconnected. Having an identity that rotates around taking care of everyone else's wants before caring for our own needs is also very unhealthy. For my growth I had to look at the people in my life and determine whether these relationships were good for me.

If you are suffering from emotional despair or unhealthy living you can begin to mend your spirit with active psychological healing techniques, positive lifestyle changes, nutrition, and even herbal medicine. Utilizing a more holistic approach can have many long-term benefits. For more information, pick up my books *Natural Mental Health* and *Learning to Say No*. For relationship issues grab a copy of *Beyond the Chase*.

Do we need to completely heal ourselves emotionally, physically, and spiritually before we can begin to make contact with the afterlife? The answer is no. If we are willing to start making healthy changes, this intention alone can begin to raise our spiritual vibration.

Along with working through my emotional baggage and caring for my physical wellbeing I began looking into what I needed to do for my spiritual health. Following are a few of the steps I took.

MY SPIRITUAL PATH

1. **Creating a spiritual sanctuary.** The first thing I needed to do was to create a private spiritual place in my home. I cleared an area in my bedroom specifically for my spiritual sanctuary. In this space I had pictures of both my departed and living loved ones. Any religious tokens such as angels, statues, candles, and holy books, or items from nature, like quartz crystals, flowers, plants, and seashells can also be included. My quiet sanctuary provided safety and enabled me to focus in on my spiritual evolution.

2. **Learning to be quiet.** My mind was so busy! Just like a squirrel in a cage! There was no room for spirituality. I learned how to turn down the volume with a simple daily meditation. After silencing the phone, and shutting off the radio, computer, and television, I'd light a candle and just stare into the flame. While I did this I'd let my mind chatter away. After several weeks I found my thoughts were beginning to slow down. Within a month the chatter was replaced with a sense of calm along with moments of enlightenment and awareness. Today when confused or stressed, I get quiet, close my eyes, and visualize my deceased loved ones. I then ask for guidance, and listen! Eventually I receive answers.

3. **Firing concepts of God or a Higher Power that don't work.** For years I was furious with God over the loss of my mother, but tried to convince myself otherwise. When I finally got honest I gave

myself permission to have my anger toward this god of my youth. Suddenly, I felt spiritually free. After firing the old god I had to find a more loving and compassionate concept. First I meditated by seeing my deceased relatives and friends in my mind's eye. Next, I asked them to show me a Higher Power I could trust and believe in. I now have a sense of spirituality that works for me.

4. **Developing religious tolerance.** When I learned I could have a relationship with a Higher Power that made sense to me, I recognized everyone had this same right. This is why there are so many different religions and spiritual philosophies. Understanding religion was manmade, but spirituality was universal, and I became more tolerant of the beliefs of others. Religion is only a path to spirituality. The path taken isn't important. How we treat ourselves and others is essential to our spiritual development.

5. **Creating personally meaningful prayer rituals.** The repetitious religious prayers of my youth were no longer comforting me. I needed something more personal. While working through my anger toward the God of my youth over my many losses, prayers for help were directed to my mother in the afterlife. I'd talk to her about my day, how I was feeling: anger, grief, fear, or sadness. Sometimes I would even draw pictures. This worked for me. Today, my form of prayer continues to include speaking from the heart with deceased relatives on the other side. Talking to a loving universal spirit initially felt awkward, so I began by writing my prayers out in a daily journal.

6. **Embracing all our emotions.** Society is quick to categorize certain human emotions as either good or bad. But in fact, feeling *all* of our feelings is healthy. How I react to my emotions can have positive or negative consequences. Unexpressed anger turns into rage, depression, or physical illness, while unresolved grief can leave us feeling hopeless. Learning how to embrace our emotions responsibly is essential. It's also important to understand that feeling numb doesn't mean we have healed ourselves. I've had some of my most powerful afterlife encounters while in the depths of emotional distress. Expressing our feelings responsibly will open us up to spiritual experiences.

7. **Accepting ourselves, warts and all.** For years I believed spiritual people were perfect people. I also thought once we physically passed we became even more perfect. For years I couldn't see how I was going to measure up. Such pressure! This kept me from trying to connect with my deceased loved ones. I'd made mistakes and I really believed this lack of perfection would disappoint them. What freed me up was recognizing that we take ourselves to the other side. This journey is just part of an ongoing process of spiritual evolution. Perfection isn't a requirement. I had to start talking to my loved ones in the next dimension just as I had when they were in this world. Along with this, if I carried anger toward any of my physically deceased family or friends, I needed to understand I could still work this out with them. And I did.

8. **Recognizing how different the physical body looks without a soul.** The fear of physical death is a Western cultural phenomenon that haunts many in our society. This also includes feeling distressed about aging: Getting physically older brings us closer to physical death! Because of these fears, there are even those who avoid visiting the elderly, the sick, or attending funerals. How can we get past this phobic behavior? When I go to funerals I'm always reminded that the physical body laid out in the casket is missing something: a soul; that "light," or a spirit. After my mother-in-law passed my then-16-year-old son wanted to see her body. When he looked down into the casket he said, "Oh! She really isn't there!" and walked away! We are not our body. Our physical self is a manifestation of our spirit. When attending a funeral, imagine the spirit of the physically deceased sitting with you, gossiping about the event! As you approach the casket for viewing, continue your conversation with the spirit of this loved one. See them standing next to you looking down on the body. In visiting the elderly or sick, look into their eyes and try to see the soul.

9. **Connecting with the soul in everyone we meet.** Each of us has a spiritual self. When friends or family hurt us sometimes it's hard to see this, but by separating the human fallibilities of those we love from their core spiritual essence we can learn to connect with others on a "soul to soul" level. Recognizing we are all spiritual creatures having a very human experience in a material world

has helped me be more forgiving and tolerant of myself and others.

10. **Studying afterlife encounters.** Looking into the history of near-death experiences, after-death communications, premonitions, and deathbed or departing visions let me know I wasn't alone in my experience. Such contact has been going on for centuries. There are also many modern-day books, online articles, weekly blogs, and Websites dedicated to afterlife encounters. When reviewing such information, my philosophy is, "Take what you like and leave the rest."

11. **Paying attention to dreams.** We can facilitate afterlife contact by paying attention to our nighttime visions and visitations from the other side. As discussed in the chapter on dreams, this isn't difficult. Looking at pictures of our physically deceased loved ones before going to sleep, and then writing out our dreams in the morning, gets this process rolling. Remember, dreams can be the doorway to a heavenly hug.

12. **Being our own medium.** We can learn to be our own medium or conduit to the afterlife. The easiest way to accomplish this is to join a Spiritualist church. These groups are typically nondenominational and open to anyone. Their philosophy is based on contact with friends and loved ones in the next dimension, and life is seen as continuous. The Website for the National Spiritualist Association of Churches is *www.nsac.org*. Even if you don't join a Spiritualist church, many groups within the NSAC offer information and even classes on mediumship.

What to Do if You Have Made Afterlife Contact

If you've had a quick peek at the next dimension or been visited by your deceased loved ones you might be asking, "How do I integrate these afterlife encounters into my daily living?"

Such experiences can rock us to our core, challenging everything we once believed. They can also pull painful issues we have avoided for years out of the darkest recesses of our mind. For example, after a series of afterlife communications, I was suddenly hit with strong feelings about a loss I had avoided addressing for a decade. Spiritual contact with a deceased loved one forced me to finally do the work to heal from this old wound.

Shortly after a departing vision, near-death experience, or afterlife communication, unresolved past traumas and losses can suddenly ambush the mind. The unfinished must be finished in order to continue exploring a spiritual path.

Along with this, after making afterlife contact we can feel alienated from our religion, friends, and even family. If people don't believe us or our experiences become the butt of bad jokes and ridicule, many of us will be at risk for isolating ourselves.

When traveling a path of spiritual enlightenment, the ride can be bumpy. On such a road we will most likely be confronted with more than one difficult spiritual lesson. Instead of sweeping these opportunities for growth under the rug, we must roll up our shirtsleeves and start beating the bushes in search of like-minded people. The Internet is a good place to start. By searching for terms like *deathbed vision*, *after-death communication*, and *near-death experiences*, not only will we find literature, but we will also find groups of people in chat rooms and on message boards eager to share what they have experienced. Once we have this support we will have more confidence in sharing openly with family, friends, and even naysayers!

Today, I have no problem letting those around me know where I stand. I don't need to sit and feel misunderstood because I've kept silent about spirituality and life after physical death experiences. If I allow this to happen, my soul feels distressed. That said, I do have boundaries of caution when there is a possible risk for experiencing unkind responses from others.

Having boundaries also means we discuss our afterlife encounters with our spouses, family, and friends without having expectations about how they will respond. They don't have to believe us or agree with us. We must also look at how we share our encounters and beliefs. Instead of trying to force our friends to accept our experiences, we will do well to just model healthy spirituality. Along with this we might want to remember how we once were before beginning our own spiritual trek.

I believe we all have an individual path to follow and specific journey in this life to complete. After experiencing a departing vision we may have a hard time recognizing where we are going. The post signs of our journey can become blurred. It's also not unusual to feel confused about the true purpose of life. What used to make sense and work for us no longer meets our needs. This can be a hard place to be in.

Afterlife experiences will force us to reevaluate our course in life. After my first series of encounters I realized

I was not happy with where I was living, so I moved closer to the sea. My work hours were too long and I was missing out on family time. Even my religion felt shallow. My priorities were no longer the same, so my lifestyle needed to change.

With spiritual growth I realized I was responsible for every aspect of my life. I had to learn how to take care of myself physically, emotionally, socially, and spiritually. It was also important to respect where my family and friends were spiritually. I needed to work on tolerance and patience while watching out for self-righteousness. Finally, I understood my life had new purpose and meaning. Because of this, I couldn't let concerns about what other people thought sway me from my path.

For thousands of years there have been tales about the departing vision. History has taught us that life continues. Our inner light can never be destroyed.

I had my first departing vision 40 years ago. Since then I've been blessed with more afterlife encounters than I can count. These blessed events have assured me that other dimensions of existence are real. When it's time for me to shed my "earthly attire" I'll be guided to the next adventure by those who have gone before me. Then together we will travel to the other side.

Though time separates one departing vision from another, the experience is the same and the message rings loud and clear: Physical death is not the end.

NOTES

CHAPTER 2

1. William, B. *Death-bed Visions: the psychical experiences of the dying*. London, Aquarian Press, 1926, pg. 27.

CHAPTER 3

1. Myers, Frederic W. H. *Human Personality and Its Survival of Bodily Death*. London: Longmans, Greens and Co., 1907, p. 193.

2. Stanton, Horace Coffin. *Telepathy of the Celestial World: Psychic Phenomena Here But Foreshadowings of Our Transcendent Faculties Hereafter.* New York: Fleming H. Revell Company, 1913, p. 348.

3. Podmore, Frank. *Studies in Psychical Research.* New York: G.P. Putnam's Sons, 1897, p. 254.

4. Lang, Andrew. *The Book of Dreams and Ghosts.* London: Longmans, Green and Co., 1899, pp. 74–75.

5. Nye, Aubrey. *Mirror Images: Is This a Genetic Link to Spirit?* Bloomington, IN: Authorhouse, 2004, p. 139.

6. Raphael, Simcha Paull. *Jewish Views of the Afterlife.* Northvale, NJ: Jason Aronson, Inc., 1994, p. 339.

7. Ibid.

8. Ibid.

9. Tabari, Watt, William Montgomery, and Michael V. McDonald. *Muhammad at Mecca.* Albany, NY: State University of New York Press, 1988, p. 71.

10. Ankerberg, John, and Emir Caner. *The Truth about Islam and Women.* Eugene, OR: Harvest House Publishers, 2009, p. 31.

11. Wright, Zachary. *On the Path of the Prophet: Shaykh Ahmad Tijani and the Tariqa Muhammadiyya.* Atlanta, GA: African American Islamic Institute, 2005, p. 51.

12. Last Words Quotations. *www.gratifying.net/last_words/quotes.htm*.

13. "Johann Sebastian Bach's Strokes." Acta Clinica Croatica (Sisters of Charity Hospital), 2006. *http://arts.pallimed.org/2009/02/johann-sebastian-bach.html*.

14. Last Words Quotations. *www.gratifying.net/last_words/quotes.htm*.

15. "10 Famous Last Words of Famous People." *www.mostinterestingfacts.com/human/10-famous-last-words-of-famous-peoples.html*.

16. Tran, Anh. "Chopin: The Poet of the Piano." *www.ourchopin.com/quotes.html*.

17. www.mostinterestingfacts.com/human/10-famous-last-words-of-famous-peoples.html

18. Finley, L. Blake, and Ruth Brummund. "Indira Gandhi: Universal Woman of Courage, Compassion, and Social Justice." *www.uranian-institute.org/brbfgandhii.htm*.

CHAPTER 4

1. Chrisholm, Hugh. *The Encyclopaedia Britannica: A Dictionary of Arts, Sciences, Literature and General Information*. Vol. 12. New York: The Encyclopaedia Britannica Co., 1910, p. 862.

2. Snell, Joy. *The Ministry of Angels Here and Beyond*. London: The Greater World Association, 1950, pp. 8–9.

3. Proceedings of the Society for Psychical Research (Great Britain), Society for Psychical

Research, London, England, Vol 34-35. Printed for the Society of Psychical Research by Robert Maclehose, Univ. Press, Glasgow. 1925. P 286.

4. Barrett, Sir William. *Death-Bed Visions: The Psychical Experiences of the Dying.* Wellingborough, UK: Aquarian Press, 1926, p. 30.

5. Osis, K., and Haraldsson, E. *At the Hour of Death: A New Look at Evidence for Life After Death.* New York: Avon Books, 1977, p. 63.

6. Ibid., p. 4.

CHAPTER 5

1. Haraldsson, E. *Synopsis: The Departed Among the Living.* Iceland: University Press, 2005.

2. Giovetti, P. "Visions of the Dead, Death-Bed Visions and Near-Death Experiences in Italy." *Human Nature* 1.1 (1999): 38–41.

3. Briggs, C. V. *World: The Ultimate Guide to Apparitions, Death Bed Visions, Mediums, Shadow People, Wandering Spirits and Much, Much More.* San Francisco: RedWheel/Weiser, LLC, 2010, p. 267.

4. Fenwick, P., and F. Santos. *Death, End of Life Experiences, and Their Theoretical and Clinical Implications for Theories of Consciousness: Exploring Frontiers of the Mind-Brain Relationship.* New York: Springer Science Business Media, 2011, p. 174.

5. Meredith, Fionola. "Going into the Light." *Irish Times*, March 3, 2011. *www.irishtimes.com/newspaper/health/2011/0322/1224292769193.html*.

6. Ibid.

7. Ibid.

8. Ibid.

9. Rockliff, Carla H. "The Hour of Departure." End of Shift: Nurses' Stories. *Nursing Spectrum*, NY/NJ edition, 2004.

10. Muthumana, S.P., M. Kumari, A. Kellehear, S. Kumar, and F. Moosa. "Deathbed visions from India: A study of family observations in northern Kerala." Abstract. *Omega (Westport)* 62. 2 (2011): 97–109. Institute of Palliative Medicine, Kozhikode, Kerala, India. *www.ncbi.nlm.nih.gov/pubmed/21375116*.

11. Societe universelle d' etudes psychiques, *Annales des Science psychiques, Recueil d'observations et d'experiences*. Paris, Alcan, F., Editor: 1891. 173. (original French)

12. Moore, Carrie A. "The Unseen Realm: Science Is Making Room for Near-Death Experiences Beyond This World." *Deseret News*, February 18, 2006.

CHAPTER 6

1. Flammarion, Camille. *The Unknown*. New York: Harper and Brothers Publishers, 1900, p. 350.

2. Perricone, Kathleen. "Weezer bassist Mikey Welsh predicted his own death in Chicago two weeks before it happened." NYDailyNews.com, October 10, 2011. *http://articles.nydailynews. com/2011-10-10/entertainment/30284588_1_ weezer-riot-fest-facebook.*

3. Ibid.

4. Ibid.

5. Munn, Michael. *X-Rated: The Paranormal Experiences of the Movie Star Greats.* London: Robson Books Ltd, Bolsover House, 1996, p. 69–70.

6. Lysette, Chantel. *Azrael Loves Chocolate, Michael's A Jock: An Insider's Guide to What Your Angels Are Really Like.* Woodbury, MN: Llewellyn Publications, 2008. 7-8.

7. Bekkum, Gary S. "Multiple Sources: CIA Knew Passenger Planes Would Be Used As Missiles Before 9/11." Before It's News, Thursday, June 14, 2012, *http://beforeitsnews.com/ conspiracy-theories/2012/06/multiple-sources-cia-knew-passenger-planes-would-be-used-as-missiles-before-911-2264004.html*

8. Bekkum, Gary S. "Parcel Bomb Plot and October Red Psychic Spy Timeline: Predicting the Next Wave of Terror Attacks." American Chronicle, November 4, 2010. *www.americanchronicle.com/articles/view/197413.*

CHAPTER 7

1. Barrett, Sir William. *On the Threshold of the Unseen: An Examination of the Phenomena of Spiritualism and of the Evidence for Survival After Death*. New York: E.P. Dutton and Company, 1918, pp. 147–148.

2. Gurney, E., Myers, F.W.H., Podmore, F. *Phantasms of the living, Volume 1*. London, Trubner and Co., Ludgate Hill, E.C., 1886. P. 560

3. Flammarion, Camille. *Death and Its Mystery at the Moment of Death*. New York, NY: The Century Co., 1922, pp. 85–86.

CHAPTER 8

1. Stonesifer, Tim. "Man, wife married 61 years, die hours apart." *The Evening Sun*, January 10, 2012.

2. Simpson, Mona. "A Sister's Eulogy for Steve Jobs." *The New York Times*, October 30, 2011. *www.nytimes.com/2011/10/30/ opinion/mona-simpsons-eulogy-for-steve-jobs. html?pagewanted=1&_r=2&sq=steve jobs*.

3. Cash, Johnny, and Patrick Carr. *Cash: The Autobiography*. New York: HarperCollins, 1997, pp. 25–27.

CHAPTER 9

1. *Journal of the American Society for Psychical Research*, Section B, Volume 12 of the *American Institute for Scientific Research*. York, PA: American Society for Psychical Research, 1918. 388.

2. Leadbeater, Charles Webster. *The Other Side of Death: Scientifically Examined and Carefully Described*. Whitefish, MT: Kessinger Publishing, 1997, p. 356.

3. Finch, Laura I., ed. *The Annals of Psychical Science: A Monthly Journal Devoted to Critical and Experimental Research in the Phenomena of Spiritism* 5 (1907): 126. London: The Annals of Psychical Science.

4. Moore, David W. "Three in Four Americans Believe in Paranormal." Gallup, June 16, 2005. *www.gallup.com/poll/16915/Three-Four-Americans-Believe-Paranormal.aspx*.

CHAPTER 10

1. Wills-Brandon, Carla. *A Glimpse of Heaven: The Remarkable World of Spiritually Transformative Experiences*. Avon, MA: Adams Media, 2004, pp. 77–81.

2. Kever, Jeannie. "Departed Loved Ones Coming Back to Say Goodbye." *The Houston Chronicle*, January 30, 2001. *www.carlawillsbrandon.com/*

*carlawillsbrandon/Essays/Entries/2009/7/16_
Departed_Loved_Ones_Coming_Back_To_Say_
Goodbye.*

3. Barrett, Sir William. *Death-Bed Visions:
   The Psychical Experiences of the Dying.*
   Wellingborough, UK: Aquarian Press, 1922, p.
   108.

4. "Excerpt from the Life, Letters, and Journals
   of Louise May Alcott. *Journal of the American
   Society for Psychical Research*, Section B 7
   (1913): 424–425.

5. Berk, Iya. "Seeing the Human Spirit Leave
   the Body at Death." Ezine Articles. *http://
   EzineArticles.com/1505048.*

6. With permission from Doc Dave to author.

7. "Stunned surgeons watch dying man's soul leave
   his body during operation!" *Weekly World News*
   16, No. 8 (1994): 40.

8. Santee, Cynthia. *The Doorway to Knowing:
   A Guide to Soulful Living.* Bloomington, IN:
   Author House, 2010, p. 57.

9. Steiger, Brad. *Real Ghosts, Restless Spirits, and
   Haunted Places.* Canton, MI: Visible Ink Press,
   2003, p. 146.

10. Ibid.

11. Degenhardt, Scott. *Surviving Death Again.* Self-
    published, 2010.

CHAPTER 11

1. Barbato, M. Reflections of a Setting Sun: Healing Experiences Around Death. Australia, Published by Michael Barbato, Griffin Press, 2009. P. 30-32

2. Nickell, Joe. "'Visitations': After-Death Contacts." *Skeptical Inquirer* 12.3 (2002). *www.csicop.org/sb/show/visitations_after-death_contacts.*

3. Kubler Ross, Elisabeth, and Todd Gold. *The Wheel of Life: A Memoir of Living and Dying.* New York: Touchstone, 1997, p. 177.

4. Kubler Ross, Elisabeth. *Death Is of Vital Importance: On Life, Death and the Afterlife.* Barrytown, NY: Station Hill Press, 1995, p. 86–87.

5. Ibid.

6. Kubler Ross, Elisabeth. *On Life After Death.* Berkeley, CA: Celestial Arts, 1991, p. 15.

7. Lattin, Don. *Expert On Death Faces Her Own Death Kubler-Ross now questions her life's work.* San Francisco, CA: San Francisco Chronicle, May 31, 1997.

Index

ABOUT THE AUTHOR

Carla Wills-Brandon has a master's degree in clinical psychology. She has researched departing-vision encounters for more than 25 years, and has published 13 books, one of which was a *Publishers Weekly* bestseller. Carla has lectured across the United States and the UK, and has appeared on numerous national radio and television programs, such as *Geraldo*, *Sally Jesse Raphael*, *Montel Williams*, Art Bell's *Coast to Coast Radio Show*, *Coast to Coast with George Noory*, Uri Geller's *Coast to Coast Radio Show*, and *Politically Incorrect* with Bill Maher. Many of her media appearances are dedicated to healing from loss.

Carla is also one of the few investigators focusing on the departing vision as proof of life after death.

Carla is married to Michael Brandon, a licensed clinical psychologist. The couple lives on the Gulf Coast in a hundred-year-old house, with their two sons and an assortment of furry pets.